Communing with the Ancestors

Communing with the Ancestors

Your Spirit Guides, Bloodline Allies, and the Cycle of Reincarnation

RAVEN GRIMASSI

WEISER BOOKS

First published in 2016 by Weiser Books, an imprint of

Red Wheel/Weiser, LLC
With offices at:
65 Parker St, Suite 7
Newburyport, MA 01950
www.redwheelweiser.com

Library of Congress Cataloging-in-Publication Data available upon request
  ISBN: 978-1-57863-593-1
  Names: Grimassi, Raven, 1951- author.
  Title: Communing with the ancestors : your spirit guides, bloodline allies,   and the cycle of reincarnation / Raven Grimassi.
  Description: Newburyport : Weiser Books, 2016.
  Identifiers: LCCN 2015047090 | ISBN 9781578635931 (6 x 9 tp : alk. paper)
  Subjects: LCSH: Spiritualism.
  Classification: LCC BF1261.2 .G75 2016 | DDC 133.9--dc23
  LC record available at http://lccn.loc.gov/2015047090

Cover design by Jim Warner
Text design by Ryan Kenney
Typeset in Warnock Pro
Cover photograph: Inukshuk monument on English Bay, Vancouver, Canada © Ian Wilson | Dreamstime.com
Spirit-Rider image by Jane Star Weils

Printed in Canada

MAR

10 9 8 7 6 5 4 3 2 1

Table of Contents

Preface

The topic of the Ancestors is not as simple as one might think. It is more than just the idea that they exist; questions arise that call for exploring much deeper. When I set out to write this book, my desire was to avoid any single cultural views or practices. I also realized that many cultures in the world today practice formal Ancestral veneration. These systems tend to be very old traditions that continue to effectively serve their practitioners well. So it was clear to me that my book was more for people exploring ways to honor and work with Ancestors. That being said, I do not avoid traditional ways, I simply focus on clearing new walkways into the Ancestral landscape.

I felt that the best approach for me in writing this book was to open myself up to the Ancestral Spirit. In general I feel that my hand is guided when I write, but in this case I came to feel that I had to get out of the way as opposed to lending my hand in the writing process. This became a very real situation for me because on the days I was left alone with the manuscript I found it a struggle to produce words of any significance to the project.

The teachings in this book came together as opposed to already being in place in one system or another. While the book draws on ancient ideas, the overall view is a descendant of them as opposed to a survival of any single tradition. In this light one can enjoy the roots as well as the new branches and fruit that are offered.

In writing this book through the Ancestral Voices I found myself having to rethink my own views. In some cases I had to abandon things I once fully integrated into my inner and outer worldviews. It is not that they were wrong or faulty; they simply did not part the curtain wide enough for a more expansive view. This yielding was not easy for me and it may not be easy for you. For myself I prefer to grow rather than to remain captive to all that I carry from past studies and experiences. In this light the book is a richer perspective from a higher vantage point—the shoulders of the Ancestors.

As my previously held beliefs were being modified, dissolved, or reconfigured in the writing of this book, I revisited the idea of belief itself. The typical dictionary defines *belief* as the mental act, condition, or habit of placing trust or confidence in another. A secondary definition is having a conviction that something is true. After some reflection on the word, I discovered that I didn't "believe" in what was being written; instead I acknowledged it at every stage.

The definition of *acknowledge* is to admit the existence, reality, or truth of something. It also means to recognize, to report receipt, and to give thanks or gratitude. With the completion of the book I feel all of those things. To feel, understand, and integrate the difference between belief and acknowledgment is a powerful gateway.

It seems there is a fount from which things of a mystical nature come to us. It is, no doubt, the same magical waters from which our Ancestors drank, and then dreamed and wrote their myths and legends. We need not rely only upon what is passed to us from preexisting sources. We who stand in the present are touched, inspired, guided, and driven by the same forces that moved our Ancestors. The old well is still there, although we quite likely need a new rope and bucket.

Throughout the book you will find various Ancestral views, beliefs, and practices. I have drawn from the oldest because I believe the roots are where nourishment is drawn. The oldest records we have are the least tampered with, and the least able to be ignored even by those determined to do so. When new ideas come flooding in and wash away the buildings and foundations, we still have the old blueprints from which to reconstruct what was lost.

My primary goal in this book is to provide pathways through which the Ancestors can regain access past the things that have stood in their way. The methods I feel they have taught me while writing this book can help their distracted descendants to hear the Ancestral Voices that offer guidance and personal empowerment. These are the voices offering peace and inner balance through returning to receptivity, returning to living in "common cause" with Nature. I caution the reader to not skim this book. It needs to be read page by page because each concept is connective and built upon another.

I fully expect that some readers will complain that I repeat material here and there throughout the book. To a certain degree this is true, but I do so to enrich the concepts through context. An old teacher of mine once said that a person can reveal all the secrets and mysteries in an afternoon, but without context no one can understand them. It will appear as gibberish. So it is not so much what is said as how and where it is said that brings the light to the surface. There was once a popular saying: "Guard the Mysteries, reveal them daily."

It is likely that the most challenging concept in the book is the material on Human Consciousness as a separate entity within what is our whole being. The hidden roots of this idea go back to the primordial world, and to those races that preexisted humankind. It is mixed in with tales of star gods, faery beings, and conflicting theological models. I found it to be a well-tangled ball of string. What I present in this book is over four months of steady work at trying to unravel what was laid at my doorstep.

Without my Ancestors, and a handful of Otherworld Allies, I do not believe this book would have been possible. Had I written it myself, I believe it would have turned out to be not unlike most published books on the Ancestors. I do not mean that in terms of quality or superiority; I mean that in terms of where one can be faery-led into the thicket. Fortunately, I was able to return with but little loss of time and just a touch more madness to my thinking.

In this book you will find the concept of the Spirit-Rider. The being, as I present it, is a blend of very old beliefs found in Mayan and Hawaiian beliefs. These beliefs are not unlike those of some old European cultures (the Scandinavian in particular). This can be seen to indicate an ancient commonality. The Spirit-Rider ties in with the Vision Serpent of Mayan culture. Here it is a serpent that delivers the spirits of the Ancestors when summoned by a priest. What I present in the book is a spiritual legacy as opposed to any specific cultural history. In other words I am using the essential concept as a mechanism, but the complete picture is something that arose within my own consciousness based upon older models.

For those who love the inner mysteries, you will find much to unravel in the pages of this book. This was certainly my own experience in walking the starlit maze that the Ancestors led me into by breath, bone, and blood. I acknowledge that your Ancestors will open the maze doors for you as well, as the concepts reveal themselves to you in the following pages.

ACKNOWLEDGMENTS

There are many people who contributed to what became this book. Some I sought out and others I chanced upon. I wish to thank Thorn Coyle for nudging me to write this book, and my wife, Stephanie, for keeping hearth and home together so that I had the time and space to create this work. Without her selfless support, suggestions, and feedback this book would not have manifested. I also want to acknowledge R.J. Stewart who taught me techniques for faery contact that ultimately opened portals to the Ancestral Realm. My thanks and appreciation also goes to Kelly Miller-Lopez for sharing her Otherworld Eyes for this vision and to Orion Foxwood for sharing his insights into Ancestral themes. Final thanks go to friends, strangers, and fellow authors such as Christopher Penczak and Ivo Dominguez who I had the privilege of talking with on this and many other topics.

Introduction

The seeds of this book were planted quite some time ago. They took root and became spectral pages of ancient memory, but this collection was left in some inner attic chest for safekeeping. To enter the attic and open the chest is to pass directly into the source. We must do more than speak the praises of that source, we must swim the depths of its current. When we emerge, only then are we worthy to read from the wisdom of the Ancestral tome that we and those who came before us have been writing all along.

Several years back, during a casual conversation with friend and fellow author Thorn Coyle, an idea arose. She suggested that I write a book on the Ancestors. As I recall we were talking about things related to that theme. Over the following years we met at various author events from time to time. Each time she brought up again the subject of writing this book. My feeling was that while I could write a nice article on the Ancestors, I did not have a book's worth in me. That is never a comfortable thought for an author, but the lessons of truth are not there for our convenience.

Thorn insisted that she could "see" this project, this book, and that I really needed to write it. It felt to me that she may have perceived a "meant to be" type of thing. I explained to her that because of our previous talks, I had gone to my Ancestors and asked about writing this book. I added that nothing came back to me from them. She suggested that I go and ask them questions, ask for a vision of the book. So I asked again, but nothing came to me.

In February of 2014, if memory serves me correctly, Thorn and I had a last discussion about the book idea. During the conversation she added that the book should be about "The" Ancestors, all of ours, not any singular bloodline. This made sense of course, and I told her that I was seriously thinking about taking on the project. Over the next few months I fell back into feeling that this book just wasn't in me, and that the Ancestors were not encouraging me to write the book.

I struggled with the idea off and on over the next couple of months. Then in the late spring of 2014 something happened to change everything. My wife and I were having breakfast at IHOP, and the topic of the book came up again. After some discussion I told her that I was not going to write the book. I repeated that the Ancestors were not sending me any message, any encouragement.

We left the restaurant, and while we were sitting in the car getting ready to drive off, a white semi-trailer truck pulled into the parking lot. It drove slowly across my view out of the front windshield. Across the huge trailer was written one word that took up the entire side of the panel; one word and one word only—it was "Ancestral." Nowhere on the trailer was there any logo, company name, or phone number. There was only the single word itself. I guess sometimes I have to be almost run over by a truck for something to get my attention.

My wife and I looked over at each other, paused in semi-disbelief (no pun intended), and then laughed out loud. She looked me in the eyes and said with a grin, "So?" I replied: "Looks like I am writing the book!" When I arrived home, I went on to the Internet to try and locate the company, the truck, or whatever I could find. Nothing came up at all except for an unrelated business over in England. The experience with the truck remains a mystery, which I suppose is as it should be.

Once I was committed to writing this book I sat down to formulate an outline so that I could propose the work to my publisher. I do not believe that I have ever had a book be exactly what I proposed and outlined, but this one turned out to be a very unique process and experience. It began as usual with me pulling some books from my library to see what others had already written on the subject. I made some notes and then turned to plan out the chapter themes.

When I write a book, I bring what I know to the project and try to add a more expanded view beyond what I have settled into as a practitioner. So I tried to write this book from what I believed I already knew about the subject and what would evolve during the writing process. This approach faltered no matter how much I pressed forward. I thought I was simply having "writer's block," so I decided to go outside for awhile and clear my head. Instead I found myself walking around in my study. I stopped in front of a bookcase and saw an old book with a piece of colored paper inserted as a book marker.

I opened the book and looked at the paper marker. It was a handwritten address that my godmother once gave me after she moved out of state. She died many years ago, and I guess I kept this piece of paper out of sentimentality. The book was one I had not looked at for well over a decade; it was on the Hawaiian Huna system. Out of curiosity I looked to see what page was marked. It was a chapter on how the conscious mind can block spiritual communication. I sat down and read the chapter; it changed everything.

The event of finding this book ushered in a series of other events. I had to stop writing the book and let the book be written. My nightly dreams included friends, family, and loved ones who had passed away. This apparently spilled over, and my wife began to dream about various deceased people in her family line on an almost nightly basis as well. The fount was flowing in abundance.

Whenever I tried to think into a chapter, the words withered away. This was something alien to me as a writer, and it was very frustrating. During the writing of this book I found myself pushed to abandon many of my previous ideas, thoughts, and beliefs on the subject of Ancestors. It was as though the Ancestors were saying that this book is about something else than what I already think I know. So I set up a mini-Ancestral shrine on my computer desk and turned the project over to the Ancestors. Every time I tried to write from my personal gnosis I became blocked. This led to what I feel was me being directed to another source outside of myself. These sources were books in my study, something said in a movie or TV show, a bumper sticker, a side comment in an unrelated conversation, and so on. It became clearer all the time that this was not my book to write.

One day I chanced upon an article written on the subject of old Scandinavian beliefs. One section addressed the idea of Three "Selves" attached to the body or spirit of a person. Although the idea of a Higher, Middle, and Lower Self is not a new concept these days, I was still intrigued. This region of the world was among the last to fall to Christianization, and in this I saw an opportunity to explore remnants that were not entirely lost to distant centuries. As I read this section, I realized that the basic ideas were almost identical to the Huna beliefs I knew from earlier studies. The destruction of old Hawaiian beliefs by Christian missionaries and the suppression of Hawaiian religion and spirituality came relatively late; it can be marked to around 1812. Like old Scandinavian beliefs, the Hawaiian old ways are not so deeply buried beneath Christian culture. We can excavate them and find less fragmented remains than in many other cultures displaced by Christianity.

The reason that any of this is important is because ancient systems reflect the beliefs of a people who lived closer to Nature. In this we see perceptions of a people less modified by advancing human culture/civilization. Instead we are looking at perceptions of the primal, or at what was birthed directly from the ancient world into the minds of our Ancestors. Political influences, strict dogma, and finite doctrine came much later. While there is as much ancient folly as there is ancient wisdom, discernment is not a lost art.

Admittedly I knew very little of Hawaiian Huna beliefs in comparison to decades of my studies in old European ones. I imagined the Huna system to be not unlike Santeria, Macumba, and other such systems. Those cultures and ways had less appeal to me in my studies, practices, and beliefs. So, in the process of writing this book I took some time to read a few more books on the old Huna perspective.

Like many people of my generation I had read books by Max Freedom Long back in the 1960s and 1970s. He wrote several books on the ways of Kahuna in Hawaii, and from his research today we have the organization known as Huna Research Associates. Popularization of the Huna system has altered its rooted ways; in many cases New Age philosophy has transformed it into a non-cultural system of positive thinking. It was for this reason that I wanted to read something written by Hawaiians who preserved the old ways, or who were connecting with them. I was directed to the work of Moke Kupihea.

Kupihea is descended from a lineage of Kahuna practitioners, and although he does not refer to himself as one, at the very least he clearly carries the heart and soul of the Kahuna. I found his writings to be very inspirational in terms of Ancestral themes. I found his way of phrasing words to be very spiritual and moving for me. As a result I have adapted some of them for my own use in communication. You will find a few of them in the pages of this book.

As previously mentioned, the old Scandinavian and Hawaiian views of the Three Selves are very close and easily match up. They present an Old World view, and an Enchanted World view, of our inner landscape as spiritual beings. I personally prefer them over modern New Age views because they go deep into our psyche in a very powerful and primal way. What I experienced through exploring these old concepts changed several of my previously held views, and shaped new models that are actually quite old ones.

In the book I spend a lot of time presenting and exploring the teachings about the Three Selves. I will quickly add that these are not the popular New Age concepts of the Higher, Middle, and Lower Selves. What I present here is an older model, an earthly rooted concept. These rooted ways help us to understand ourselves as non-material beings and how to better function in a material reality. This might not be the material that one expects from a book on the Ancestors, but because our Ancestors are an important part of our inner selves and our spiritual journey, the material is indeed very relevant.

Two chapters in the book deal with reincarnation, death, and the process of the return of the soul. In those chapters you will discover teachings about the role of the Ancestors in those processes; you will also see the relationship between the soul on one plane of existence and the Ancestor on another. Related to this is the teaching on why souls are drawn to specific bloodlines. One of the goals of this book is to stir new thought while at the same time building upon rooted ideas that are strong and enriching. To that end the sections on reincarnation draw together concepts that are integrated into an alternative to commonly held views on the topic. The book presents a "start to finish" look at the process and purpose of reincarnation (and the role that the Ancestors play in it).

Writing this book brought me many teachers in order for it to come together in the way it needed to take form. Some of them I feel were my own Ancestors and the newly dead who surround me—old friends and my mother. However, there was also one who I cannot truly define or assign to my life and personal lineage. I call this entity "The" Ancestral Spirit. It brought out a non-cultural understanding underlying the views of individual cultural expressions.

The basic idea of the Ancestors is that they stay in contact with their living descendants. They are, through a process we will later explore, attached to family lines and to individuals within bloodlines. However, people who describe past life memories often depict themselves as having lived in different cultures. For example, a person might recall once being an ancient Egyptian, a Celtic warrior, an African witch doctor, and a Spanish pirate. If reincarnation allows one to jump around like that, how do the Ancestors stay connected through time to a specific lineage if the traveler does not? In writing this book these were the types of questions and thoughts I experienced in the process. They guided me through a spiritual maze that was well worth the effort.

Perhaps the most profound experience in writing this book is that I became a student to it. I passed from being in my collective knowledge to participating with the spirits who previously directed me to that storehouse of knowledge.

I realized the difference between writing from my own sense of "personal correctness" and writing from the reason I spent all these years gathering in the grain, so to speak. In the final analysis I feel that why we do things is of equal if not more importance than how we do it. It may not be the best working model for daily life, but I feel it is an excellent one for inner spirituality.

In addition to being a book on the Ancestors it is also one on associated spirituality. In this light the book is about the journey of the soul and its connection to Ancestral lines. I hope it will be a catalyst to books being written by other authors willing to take it to the next level down the road. There are so many different views of the Ancestors, perhaps as many views as there are individual people. This should not separate us; instead it should bring our visions together for a broader understanding.

In the pages of this book you will find things that are controversial and challenging as well as empowering and foundational. There are mystical elements that the average reader may find difficult to embrace. Once example is the teaching about a particular form used by an Ancestor that attaches itself to a person in a specific lifetime. This is reminiscent of what we find in shamanic tales of transformation into animal forms—the shapeshifter. Another challenging element is the association of serpents with the Ancestors. Western culture typically views the serpent with negativity and uses its form to denote danger or treachery. However in this book the Ancestral view of the serpent is redeemed, pointing to such things as the twin serpents on the caduceus, which is a symbol of health and enlightenment.

The concept of redemption itself, or of healing, is a recurring theme in the book. This is rooted in the teaching that some of our Ancestors need to be released from the energy of misdeeds performed in a lifetime. This is not only connected to a grievous wrongdoing by an Ancestor but also of serious wrongs perpetrated against her or him. The energy of such deeds can remain with us after death and bind us from being able to move on.

A theme that is growing in popularity—The Living River of Blood—is explored in several chapters. I present it as a current of energy that flows from each generation through time. Many people regard it as a stream of consciousness emanating from the Ancestral pool. The general idea is that the Ancestors can be contacted, or connected with, through the River of Blood. If the theme strikes a chord with you, and you want additional information, then I recommend the works of R.J. Stewart and Orion Foxwood for a deeper exploration of the topic.

The core theme of my book is that the Ancestors are conscious beings. They constitute the human line that is of the earth and connected to it. The teachings I present separate souls from human beings, and further separate the physical body from the consciousness of the person inhabiting it. For the purposes of the book Human Consciousness is referred to as the personality or persona.

The typical dictionary defines *person* as the composition of characteristics that make up an individual personality. The word *personality* is further defined: a person as the embodiment of distinctive traits of mind and behavior. Both words are ultimately derived from the Latin word *persona*, which means a mask or a role. This strongly reflects the idea that our human self is actually covering something else that we truly are behind it (just as a face mask hides our identity). In the context of the book, the soul is wearing the personality much like a person attending a costume party. Staying in role is part of the experience, but at some point the mask must be discarded.

The soul is often defined as that which animates the personality and is the immortal being within the body. This suggests that the persona or personality is indeed a separate entity from that of the soul and the body. We can liken this to understanding the difference between the brain and the mind. The brain masks the mind through appearing to be the lead character. However, the mind directs the brain; the brain provides the mechanism through which consciousness is fixed to a physical form. It is like a microphone for the voice; without it the voice is diminished by space, but the voice still exists even when the microphone malfunctions or is turned off.

In this book I treat the body as a separate and sentient being. This is actually a very old belief among primitive tribal people, which again speaks to me of important primal roots. I do not dismiss evolved ideas or philosophical ones; I find them useful for exploring and examining the higher elements of our being as spiritual entities. I just think that primal ideas are more effective at revealing matters of material existence. They are closer to the flesh if you will. So in this light the flesh body is called the Elemental Body. It is formed from the processes within the Elemental Plane of Existence. As described in this book, that process is overseen by the Ancestors. Here we are dealing with the "as above, so below" teaching as it relates to DNA. This is a teaching stating that every material object or principle has a non-material counterpart operating on a higher plane. So the point here is that there is spirit-like DNA and material DNA. One is directed by the Ancestors, which generates what will become a formation of energy. The other one becomes a formation that will generate a Material Body. The latter is ultimately directed by the descendants who procreate.

One difficult concept that emerged while writing this book is that of the origins of Human Consciousness (or more accurately the origins of humans as beings). What was passed to me is the idea that this goes back to the tales of star beings who came down to Earth and created humans. Almost all primitive cultures have myths of this kind. Whereas the soul can be ascribed to creation by that which created all things, what about the creation of humankind that followed? In working with this idea I came to see humans as the Clay race and souls as the Star race.

Gerald Massey, a 19th-century writer on Egyptian mythology, points to the creation of humans as originating from the Elements. He talks about the Seven Elements of ancient Egyptian thought, listing them as Darkness, Light, Breath (Air), Water, Earth, Fire, and Blood. Massey goes on to say that humans were made from the last Element, that of blood. He adds that the blood was that of a virgin maiden, but he does not provide any identifying details. We can assume that because humans did not exist at the time of this creative blood that it must be non-human.

Proponents of the theory that space aliens visited the earth in the past, and either created or genetically altered humans, may find the following to be of interest. Scientists have discovered new stem cells, dubbed endometrial regenerative cells, in the menstrual blood of women. They are unique in that they reproduce faster than other stem cells in the body, and have a better adaptability to become anything in the body. With these stem cells there is a reduced chance of rejection by a flesh body when the cells develop into something specific. In this light, alien intervention enthusiasts might be excited to think of the possibility that such cells were used to generate humans from alien blood through genetic engineering. This is not my position, but it is an interesting thought to play with while sitting in a waiting room.

Using the old myths of Egypt, Massey depicts the creative period of Earth as producing life-forms that were "bound up" together; they were the same animistic nature power. He states that at one point humankind reached a distinction between other life-forms on Earth. Massey adds that this separated humans forever from the mysterious relationship and bond of unity; they could no longer return to the "soul" of the animal, fish, bird, and reptile.

Among the ideas put forth by Massey, he introduces the tales of a Star race known as the Watchers. He draws upon the ancient Book of Enoch in which we find these *beings* assigned to seven primary powers (suggestive of a link to the Seven Elemental Forces in the mythos provided by Massey). One feature of the Watcher tale is their association with the biblical lore in which the "sons of god" mate with human women and produce offspring. To borrow a line from *Alice in Wonderland*, things get "curiouser and curiouser."

Earlier I mentioned my personal vision about the Clay race and the Star race (in thinking of us as being comprised of the consciousness of both). When the two are joined together, they share one consciousness, which is strongly suggested by the fact that we talk to ourselves, that we have internal dialogue. If there is only "one of us" inside, then there is no reason or need for internal disagreements or debates! However, our Human Consciousness is often in internal conflict. Psychology looks at the human mind as being comprised of the conscious and subconscious factions.

This treats humans as though they are schizophrenic-like beings. Might it be instead that humans are beings that host a higher consciousness that is not human? In some systems of belief such as the Huna, communication within us is assigned to three separate beings that interact: body, mind, and soul.

In many schools of thought the body and Human Consciousness dissolve after death, but the soul continues to exist. However, if Human Consciousness is obliterated, then does this not negate a direct connection to the Ancestors? If souls reincarnate, and live many lives in different genetic bodies, how do the Ancestors continue in a stream of consciousness to their descendants? Who is at home in the body to receive them—a familiar soul or a stranger?

Such questions lead me back to thinking of humans as a separate race, beings that are separate from the body and the indwelling soul. This train of thought became somewhat science fiction-like in the consideration that one of us (body, mind, or soul) might be an alien! As mentioned earlier, some very old cultures seem to be telling us that humans were created by gods who came to Earth (not THE god, but the gods). If we accept that souls were created before humans, then in effect there are two different races.

In the old Huna belief there is a suggestion that humans, as a people or race, belong to a pool of consciousness. In essence, after death, Human Consciousness returns to this pool and is drawn out again to embody a descendant. This is not an official Kahuna teaching per se; it is an elaboration passed to me as I read the old Hawaiian myths that Moke Kupihea wrote about in his books. He would likely disagree with my interpretation, or perhaps he might grin with a secret inner knowing. I like to think it would be the latter.

During the course of working with the Ancestral Spirit on this book, a variety of ideas about an Ancestral Realm arose. However, they varied in significant ways from most found in popular myths and legends. In other words they did not mesh well with pre-fashioned concepts about feasting halls, Ancestral banquets, Elysian Fields, the Summer Land, the Underworld, merrily dancing around the throne of "God" in adoration, or sitting in an honored place aside the gods in a cloud city. What I envisioned is a dimension, a place or zone connecting the past and present together. I see it as one of the in-between places that our Ancestors believed were magical or mystical realms.

This Ancestral Realm can be thought of as containing the collective spirit of all departed humans. Think of this as the past, holding the memory of its time along with the life energy of the people of a particular land (or even culture). We can liken this to a containment field. Human Consciousness, when without a body, resides in this field. The Ancestors direct individuals out from the field into a new human body. An Ancestor accompanies an individual, or several, coming and going between the world of the Living and the Ancestral Realm as need be.

In contrast to Human Consciousness the soul is depicted as entirely celestial in nature. It does not originate from the earth. From a mystical perspective the soul is said to originate amidst the stars. Throughout the book this metaphor is maintained in connection with the soul. However, in connection with reincarnation, other realms such as the Lunar Sphere are linked to the soul. This is primarily by way of addressing the soul as transcending into non-material realms as it evolves from lifetime experiences in the Wheel of Rebirth.

All of the tenets in this book coalesce in the chapter on connective rituals. None of the rites are taken from preexisting outside sources. However, in terms of the Ancestral shrine, because of the commonality of cultural practices associated with a shrine, similarities were unavoidable. The section on the Ancestral Altar contains the core idea depicted in previous books I have written, but the rite is different enough to spare the reader from another rehash of the same material. I have included other rites for the blessing of an infant/child and a funeral rite.

The chapter on connective rites also contains rituals that work with more esoteric themes and natures. One ritual is designed to heal Ancestral wounds, and another is crafted to summon an Ancestor into shared consciousness (of a temporary nature). I have also included a rite to quell discords we have with other souls in this lifetime—in other words, with people we have wronged or who wronged us. The ritual helps dissolve the disharmony and to release fault.

Although this work is titled a book on the Ancestors, it is in addition a journey taken with them. We are not alone in this lifetime; we are accompanied. There are voices whispering to us from within our blood. These are the Ancestors who have lived lives before us and want to share the benefits of their experiences. You and I have been called back into physical life for a purpose. Yes, your life has a purpose and a reason for being in this time and place. Listen to those who discovered this in their own lifetimes and now see things from the other side of life with greater understanding.

CHAPTER 1

SPIRITUAL HEIRLOOMS

I perch upon the old tales of my Ancestors. Not all of them are recorded in myth, legend, or ballad. I hear now, as I have for most of my life, the inner stories whispered to me by my Ancestors. I do not find them to be less than the published books containing recorded Ancestral ways, beliefs, and stories. These printed tales themselves originated from an earlier "inner knowing" before any Ancestor or descendant ever penned them on paper. Some memories are recorded, some flow silently within the blood, and others are carried on the Voice of the Wind.

My eyes look out upon a modern world but see an ancient one. Our lineage is spiritual; it is an heirloom preserved within us. Your soul and mine, in many bodies, once walked upon the Ancestral lands, tread over the bones of our dead, and stood in the center of what our Ancestors once knew as sacred. Through various people, our souls have witnessed what is often called history, as well as all that escaped the attention of history and historians over the ages.

Old primitive stories tell us that the Ancestral gods came to Earth and scattered bits of flame from within themselves, which went on to become the human race. These spirit flames that were passed from the gods then flowed through the generations of humans that followed this ancient time and mystical event. Perhaps the heart of this theme is reflected in the custom of people seated before a fire sharing stories and family tales.

The Ancestral flame is inherent in each living generation; its light is within you at this very moment. It can illuminate the past, present, and future if you carry it there.

Stars were once thought of as flickering flames in the night sky. Here the mythical Seven Sisters danced in the Pleiades, and from their influence mortals created the rites of night. These descending daughters of May are the departing daughters of November's Eve; they are half-sisters to the Hesperides who tend the garden in which the fruit of immortality grows and is guarded by a serpent. These Seven Daughters of Night are also half-sisters to Hermes who escorts the Dead. There is more to say about all of this in a later chapter.

Death is inevitable. As the last breath of our body leaves us, we go out with it to the mountaintop that looks out upon the realm of our Ancestors. At birth, with the first breath of our new body, our Ancestors have returned us to the world of mortalkind. Once free of the womb to draw that breath, we cry out with sorrow, knowing that our feet fell short of reaching the Hidden Realm, and we also cry out with astonishment at the road we must travel once again in the flesh; the way to the Ancestors and to the starry path beyond. When newborns wail, pathways open.

It is the life breath that unites us with our Ancestors. On our breath is carried the memories of them when we speak about those who came before us; on our breath is carried the prayers and chants that we raise for the Ancestors. Breath passes through the blood within our lungs, and in our blood is the connection back to bone; back to all that comes from within the bone. The Ancestors are the marrow of the bone memory. Breath allows the Ancestors to rise within us and for us to submerge within them.

*If we are reborn
we ARE the
ancestors*

In the human fetus, marrow first appears in the clavicles (the collarbones). The name *clavicle* comes from the Latin word for "little key" and is descriptive of the shape of the bone, which looks much like an old-fashioned skeleton key. Within bone marrow is a membrane that prevents cells that have not matured from passing into the greater body through the bloodstream. In metaphysics there is also a "membrane" that prevents immature souls from eluding the Wheel of Rebirth and slipping into the greater body of Reality. Guardians and keys are always present at the gates between life, death, and renewal.

When our breath carries the words we speak to someone about our Ancestors, they hear us on the Voice of the Wind. The Ancestors are said to travel out upon our life's breath, which carries them into the next generation when their stories continue to be passed on from generation to generation. If we are faithful bearers of "the story," then we too are carried upon the breath of the Living when we pass from the world of mortalkind through the Gate of Death.

In the book *The Cry of the Kahuna*, Moke Kupihea describes himself as a "hereditary scribe" serving the Ancestral Voices of his lineage. This can be true for all of us if we choose to take on this role. The arm and the reach of our Ancestors is very long; its elbow is pressed into the past, its forearm extends into the present, and its hand reaches to touch the future.

It seems that many people think of the Ancestors as being something entirely of the past. This view can extend to thinking of the Ancestors as part of a dead and distant world, half-remembered if remembered at all. However, the Ancestors are conscious beings, and they are not detached from the world of the Living. We can touch them and talk with them because they are everywhere. They are part of the land, for they have passed into it; they are part of the air because their life breath was joined to it. When we remember the Ancestors, we literally "bring them to life" because they enter into us who are the living generation.

Walk upon the ancient sites, pause amidst the old standing stones, and touch the once sacred waters. In doing so, you can come to the realization that the Ancestors are part of the landscape as well as the dreamscape. Interface with your Ancestral land and you meet the first Ancestor. You will return to your origins. Looking up from the first altar set by the first Ancestor, you can see the stars, the moon, and the sun anew. Interface with your dreamscape and you will enter into the presence of the Source of All Things.

You exist today in the material world because each of your direct Ancestors lived long enough to procreate. The seeds scattered by the Ancestors have become you; you are the sprout and the future seed-bearer of your lineage. You may choose not to procreate or you may not be able to do so. This need not end your role in passing on the seed-lineage because your soul can return to the bloodline again in a future lifetime. There are many byways that cross the sacred landscape.

The landscape of our Ancestors presented a much richer vision than that of modern humans. They knew of older races on the earth before the reign of humankind. One of them was the Faery race. The old tales and ancient beliefs cast a mystical mist, and in its periodic parting we catch glimpses of Faery mounds, secret lake islands, and doorways to the Hidden Realm itself. In the mixing and overlapping lore, the lines blur between Neolithic burial mounds and Faery mounds, and even between faeries and spirits of the Dead. In the gathered mist the world of the Dead, that of the Faery, and the realm of the Ancestors becomes almost indistinguishable.

Among our Ancestors were the seers, those with what is often called the Second Sight. They saw that the Sacred landscape was both material and non-material. In this light the realm of Faery is the inner landscape of Nature. Because humans are a part of Nature, a threshold to the realm of Faery exists within us as well. It is an inner place and so it cannot readily be seen through the physical eyes unless they look through the heart of the innermost self. Perhaps this *is* the Second Sight, the moving away from the physical eyes to their counterparts that see the landscape in our dreams.

Dreams are footpaths and portals to the Otherworld. The dreamscape colors the myths and legends passed to us from our Ancestors. It adds the imagery that connects the world of mortalkind to the eternal world that is its counterpart. Through the old stories we find a mirroring. Just as a forest or a city is reflected upon a lake or another body of water (in reversed position) so too it is with the outer and inner worlds. Bodies of water mirror the upper world of humankind and suggest a parallel realm beneath in which the spiritkind dwells. Thoughts of other lands, other worlds, have always compelled exploration.

Mystical passageways and inner realms are featured in most tales of quest. In them the hero is gifted an object (or obtains it through self-effort) that makes success possible in completing the goal. In Northern Europe one example is the Silver Bough, a magical apple branch with silver apples on it. This is given to the hero by a Faery Queen, and it grants safe passage to and from the realm of Faery. In Southern Europe the object is the Golden Bough, a mystical oak branch with mistletoe on it. This bough allows safe passage to and from the Underworld. Both of these myths or legends point to a belief that once a mortal enters the inner realm, no return is normally intended in any way that is natural to that realm.

The stories of our Ancestors tell us that the Otherworld Realm is a land "fairer than any known to mortals." In this land it is always Summer, with clear flowing water and breezes perfumed with the scent of flowers. The meadows are always in blossom, and the trees are hung with ripened fruit. Birds are in song, and honey is abundant simply for the taking. From time to time the beautiful sound of a harp with silver strings drifts by and stirs love in the youths and maidens who enjoy this wondrous realm.

The faeries who were known to our Ancestors were not the small winged beings sitting on flower tops as seen on modern greeting cards. Some old tales depict them having a fair complexion and their long yellow hair is fixed back with combs of gold. They wear a mantle of green cloth inlaid with wild flowers; their pants are green and they wear silver shoes. In one disquieting description the faeries carry quivers of "adder slough" and their bows are made of human ribs, which are taken from graves where the lands of three lords come together. Their arrows are made from bog reed, tipped with white flints that are dipped in the dew of hemlock. The faeries ride on steeds whose hooves do not disturb the meadow flowers. This is quite a different depiction of faeries from that of modern minds.

Other accounts, such as those of Robert Kirk in the 17th century, provide a wider view of the Faery race. His journal depicts the faeries as consisting of tribes and orders. Kirk refers to faeries as the Sith (Sidhe) and separates them into "good" and "bad" in terms of their interactions with humans. He writes that the Sith are divided into two different courts known as the Seelie and the Unseelie. The former title means "blessed," and the latter means "unblessed." Kirk describes the land of the faery as being similar to the human world with its own terrain and light. However, time is different in their realm and is not measured in the way of humankind; the cycles and tides of their enchanted landscape have their own rhythm.

The inner and outer landscape of our Ancestors was vital because it connected them with the tides and cycles of not only Nature, but also the Cosmos. Renewal and continuation were the lessons taught each year as the Four Seasons gave way to one another during the course of the year. This pattern extended to erecting standing stones designed to track celestial events. Through this, humankind learned it could participate in the repeating patterns, and that it belonged to something greater.

Great emphasis was placed upon the family and tribe. Rituals and customs grew around these units. One old practice was for a baby to be brought to the oldest matriarch. She would look into the eyes of the baby to see if she could recognize a reincarnated member. A return to the bloodline was considered to be an important event as we will see in later chapters of this book. One related practice was to name newborns after someone who had passed into the Otherworld. This was intended to honor the memory of the individual, but it is also a stepping stone between the past and the present.

Memory is an important connective element in the theme of the Ancestral Spirit. We see this even in simple ways such as keeping photos of departed loved ones on the fireplace mantle or somewhere in the home. This practice may come from more than just the desire to remember them; the Ancestors do not want to be forgotten. They influence us in ways that escape the attention of a great many people.

In days of old it was a common practice for people to try to fulfill what a loved one had not completed in her or his life. In part this was believed to help the deceased "rest in peace," but there is another larger idea underlying the quest. What I refer to here is the Ancestral Mission, the collective goal of a lineage. Just as individuals work to create change in their lifetime, to make a difference, so too does the Ancestral Spirit. Each newborn member of a lineage is seen as another agent sent to help accomplish the goal. This ties into the three components of living one's life, all of which are ultimately connected to the Ancestral Spirit.

The Threefold Currents of Life

Humans have long pondered the question as to whether or not life has any meaning. Is there purpose? Do our lives matter in the larger picture? Is our existence just a fluke? All of these questions are strongly egocentric and seem to bypass the higher thought that our existence is part of a larger theme. In one sense this is like a skin cell wondering about the meaning of its existence as though there is no body in which it lives, operates, and functions.

One view that can help to try to sort this out is the idea of three components to life in the material world. They are called Participation, Being, and Purpose. Each has its own polarity of active and passive, projective and receptive. While each one can stand apart, there is greater realization in understanding them as three parts of a single whole. Integrating them helps create a state of consciousness that is conducive to communicating with the Ancestors. That is to say, it builds internal bridges between our body, mind, and spirit, which in turn allow for full access by the Ancestral Spirit entering into our consciousness.

While there is no particular order for the components, let us begin with Being. This is the state of awareness of one's environment through which existence is the acceptance of life itself. To embrace Being is to not question in the moment. We are, instead, basking within the gift of pure being. We can liken this to sinking into a genuine warm hug from someone we love; it is an enveloping feeling and not something thought out or pondered in the moment. We cannot sustain our daily lives in that mindset, but we should accept there is a reality that does not call for questions or discernment. It exists, and unlike all other relationships, it asks nothing of us in return.

The Gift of Being is to know for even just a fleeting moment that life is its own answer. When we are in Being, there is no expectation, no disappointment, no gain and no lack, no need or desire. One might say that this is what we glimpse through the things we hold as sacred. It is the soul's sanctuary; it is the place of rest from the demands of the human condition.

The next component is Participation. This is the savoring and the appreciation of the Gift of Pure Being through action within our lives. We can observe this in the reactions of small children who are experiencing anew the world in which we live. They can have such wonder at the things we have come to take for granted or minimized to the point that we no longer give them any meaningful attention (if we give them attention at all).

When a child looks upon the world, everything enters her or his consciousness through the eyes. The features in this world, the sky, the land, the flowing waters, the lakes and oceans, are the things once known to our Ancestors. Those who came before us are imprinted in the Spirit of the Land, and through this their life shines forth into the eyes of the child. As these things become the memory of the child, the Ancestors climb them like the rungs on a ladder. This joins the Ancestors to the child, and he or she is watched and guided as the child enters into participation with life.

Participation is Human Consciousness (as opposed to the soul's consciousness) operating within the material world within a lifetime. This participation is analytical, questioning, methodical, and discerning (in ways that are both impeccable as well as flawed). Left to its own devices Human Consciousness can turn participation into victimization, abandoning self-responsibility and laying all blame upon others. This is why we must embrace Being and Participation, which can then lead us further into the enriching currents of life.

The last component is Purpose, which is the acknowledgment of oneself as a part of a greater whole, or in service to a greater whole. Of the three components of the Current of Life, this one is most connected to the Ancestral Spirit. This is because we share this phase of consciousness with our Ancestors; they have a vested interest in how we live our lives. This is because they have a mission to accomplish through us, just as we have goals we want and need to reach. Purpose inspires us to quest within our inner being, and to quest within the outside world that surrounds us.

Throughout the chapters of this book you will encounter teachings about the Three Selves that make up our overall being. The consciousness of the Three Selves works in tandem with the Three Currents of Life. Each self is separate, independent but reliant upon the others, and each one embarks on a journey intended to result in enlightenment and evolution. Through this interconnected three-way communication the Ancestors build bridges to memory within us. We return through our Ancestors back to the place of our

in singular control. The passenger is the elderly parent in the car who has well-traveled the road but whose experience and advice is not always welcome or accepted. The desired alternative is to work well together on the journey and arrive at the destination enriched for the effort.

The Ancestors belong to the line of Human Consciousness. They maintain the ancient pool of flames, and they keep the way open to and from it. Our Ancestors are stewards of the earth and the Spirit of the Land. They are beneath the soil living in the roots and sending up sprouts. They move between the worlds and show us who we are by reminding us of what shaped us in the past. They offer us a flaming torch when all artificial lights fail to show us the way ahead.

The Ancestral Spirit moves about in the shadows cast by the flickering flames of torch and hearth. Those who came before us give life to ancient memory. They glide across the threshold that separates past and present. The Ancestors watch from the in-between places. They carry with them the essence of a time when humankind lived in common cause with Nature. The Ancestors give life to memory, and they ask us to recall.

CHAPTER 2

Ancestors

Old Lore and Memories

Not long after moving from California to New England I noticed old cemeteries nestled in neighborhoods and along the roadsides. In California cemeteries are rarely in a location where they can be seen during normal travel. It is as if they don't exist, and the running joke is that this is because no one ever dies in California. It is the land of eternal youth.

In New England I have walked through many old cemeteries. The dates on the headstones are very old, many of them going back to before the Revolutionary War between the United States and England. Here we find that stones remember what people have long forgotten. The city of the Dead is lined with silent paths that wander among the long unvisited graves.

Stones share a long and intimate history with humankind. Prehistoric graves often include stones once carried by wandering humans from their original lands. This suggests a strong tie back to origins or sense of place. Our Ancestors erected what are now mysterious "standing stones" at various ancient sites. They also left paintings on stone walls inside caves. Stone has preserved the memory of those who lived ages ago; vague though their message may be to us in modern times.

Perhaps in no place more than cemeteries does stone contain the memory of the Dead. When we think of cemeteries, we tend to think about people being counted among the Dead. It is less common for cemeteries to readily invoke the idea of our Ancestors, and this is particularly true in terms of the survival of consciousness. Cemeteries are places of the Dead. Later in this book we will find the places of the Ancestors.

At this point you may be wondering about the difference between the Dead and the Ancestors. From a metaphysical perspective the Dead become Ancestors when no presently living person knew or experienced them in his or her own life. In other words, if no one alive today personally remembers your great grandmother, then she is an Ancestor. The people you personally knew in life who have died are now the Dead. In other chapters of this book we will explore the process of death, the separation of the spirit and the soul, and many other concepts.

Lineage, in terms of remembering and acknowledging our Ancestors, is often set into a design that is called *The Family Tree.* It is interesting that a symbolic tree is used in connection with those who have gone before us. In old lore, trees are associated with the Dead, and by extension with the Ancestors. Certain trees such as the cypress, willow, and yew are intimately connected with the Dead. They commonly appear in cemeteries more than any other type of tree (with the possible exception of the oak). You might think that trees are planted in cemeteries primarily to provide beauty and shade for visitors or simply to keep erosion of the soil as bay. However, our Ancestors had a more "Otherworld" notion about trees.

An old view was that the Dead passed into trees when they separated from their flesh bodies. Another belief held that spirits of the Dead could be bound to trees if planted over their graves. Ancient myths and legends tell of humans that the gods transformed into trees. Other myths inform us that humans were made from trees, particularly the ash tree. In Southern Europe tales relate that Zeus made the "brazen race of men" from ash trees, and in Northern Europe humans were produced from the World Tree known as Yggdrasil, which was a giant ash tree. In this we can see a very primal theme. It may have originated (in part) from the lingering memory of human Ancestors having once been forest dwellers.

Another tree associated with the Dead is the birch tree. In old lore, spirits of the Dead dress in vests and hats made of birch. The white birch is sometimes viewed as an Otherworld tree or a Faery Realm tree. White is often associated with the faery places, and the white horse is a prominent feature among faery beings. White transports the Dead; white is the Gateway of Death. It opens to reveal the bone memory of all who ever lived upon the earth.

The full moon glowing white in the night sky is intimately connected to spirits of the Dead. The writings of scholar Franz Cumont contain a variety of studies that show the widespread veneration of the Dead and of the Ancestors. The connection to the moon is noteworthy. According to Cumont, the theme of the Dead and the moon appears in European, Indian, Eastern, and African cultures. He states that one of the earliest references appears in the ancient Upanishads: "All who leave the earth go to the moon, which is swollen by their breath during the first half of the month." Symbols of the moon appear in funeral monuments among the ancient Babylonian and Sumerian cultures. The crescent figure appears frequently in ancient Celtic tomb markings.

Cumont comments that at some point the Dead were also associated with the stars. He notes the ancient belief that each person has her or his star in the night sky. Its brightness or dimness denotes the life experience. When the person dies, the star falls from the sky:

> *There was also a very widely held belief, which has survived in European folklore, that each man has his star in the sky. This star is dazzling if his lot be brilliant, pale if his state of life be humble. It is lit at his birth and falls when he dies. The fall of a shooting star therefore denotes a person's death.*—After Life in Roman Paganism, *page 92*

The ancient Pythagoreans believed the soul was celestial in origin, and that its fiery spark descended at birth into a body. Aristophanes writes of seeing a new star in the sky and asking the question: "Is it true that when someone dies he becomes like a star?"

Not all cultures depicted the Dead as departing the Earth; some of them envisioned the Dead as being tied to graveyards or wandering the Earth. In this view the Dead required food and drink as did the Living. Offerings were made to them by family and loved ones. This was also performed to ensure the goodwill of the Dead. One belief held that the neglected Dead could cause harm to the Living. Various ailments and tragedies experienced by families were attributed to angry or offended spirits of the Dead.

Caring for the Dead is an important aspect associated with Ancestral veneration. Highly featured in Chinese and Japanese cultures is the preparation of the Dead and rites of purification. In some Buddhist customs family members return to Ancestral places for a family reunion, and they join together to visit their Ancestors' graves. One shared belief is that the spirits of the Ancestors revisit the household family altars during this period.

In India the Ancestors are venerated during a sixteen-day period occurring in September and October that includes food offerings. Contemporary European celebrations associated with the Dead take place at the close of October and the beginning of November. This period is often called All Souls Day, and can be regarded as a remnant of old Pagan festivals such as Samhain. Traditional Gaelic rites occur on the Eve of November in Wales, Ireland, and Scotland. At this time the veil between the worlds is said to thin or part, which allows the Dead (and the Ancestors) to return to the world of the Living.

A Mexican festival known as *Día de Muertos* (Day of the Dead) is held on November 1 to honor the Dead. Public altars are placed in community areas to honor departed loved ones. They are decorated with colorful flower arrangements, religious symbols, and vividly painted skulls. Small images of skeletons are included in the décor, and these figures are dressed in attire suited to various social occasions. Wedding attire is a very popular example when these figures are present.

The use of altars, festivals, offering, and acts of veneration all point to a belief that the Living and the Dead are in an active, ongoing relationship. This is strongly suggested in the belief that the Dead return at specific times, and that offerings are accepted by them. This is a conscious agreement, and both the Living and the Dead participate in the continuing festivals and celebrations. This raises the question: Where are the Ancestors when they are not with us?

Many religions teach that the Dead enter a permanent realm such as "heaven" or "hell." However, people died in ages before humans established religions or religious beliefs. We may well ask: What happened to the Dead in prehistoric times? The logical answer is that what happened is what happens naturally. On one level in Nature, dead bodies decompose within the soil; but we are more than just bodies, we are also energy. One teaching is that the body and the energy of the person enter into the Organic Memory of the Earth. Here all things are remembered and stored (not unlike the idea of a hard drive in a computer).

The basic idea of the Organic Memory of the Earth suggests that whatever remains of us is bound within the earth. Such a view does not take into account that although we are born on the Earth Plane we originate from a non-material realm. One relevant ancient text appears in the Orphic Tablets (tablet of Petelia) dating from the 3rd century BCE, which provides instructions for the Dead, and reads:

> *You will find to the left of the house of Hades a well-spring and by the side thereof standing a white cypress. To this well-spring approach not near. But you shall find another by the Lake of Memory, cold water flowing forth, and there are Guardians before it. Say 'I am a child of Earth and of Starry Heaven. But my race is of Heaven alone. This you know yourselves. And so I am parched with thirst and I perish. Give me quickly the cold water flowing from the Lake of Memory' and of themselves they will give you to drink from the holy well-spring.*

In this text we see the teaching that we are of another race, the race of the stars. Our celestial nature cannot be bound for long to the Material Body or the Material Realm. Therefore the soul is not permanently bound to the Organic Memory of the Earth. That being said, it is a metaphysical teaching that things remain connected through an energy field. Modern biologists such as Rupert Sheldrake refer to this as a morphogenetic field. This field of energy is generated by organic life-forms and serves to maintain communication. In this light a group of individuals that share company are connected through metamorphic fields that relay information to all members. Even when a member moves to a distant location, he or she is still connected to the group members through the field. It requires an intentional severance to disrupt the field and disconnect the member.

One primitive example of the mechanism of a morphogenetic field is a belief found among some magic users. It holds that a hair clipping, fingernail, or an unwashed article of clothing can be used to affect the person of origin. This is because a thread of energy remains that connects and ties this all together, which makes it possible to communicate through the etheric thread that runs through energy fields.

If we apply the idea of metamorphic fields to Ancestral spirits, we can consider that contact and communication are possible. The biology is still there because one half of the team is still among the Living. The living generation has within its bodies the bits of matter and energy passed on by the Ancestral line through the replication of DNA. In this light, no true break or disconnect exists. Even in the case of adoptees, the Ancestral connection is still in the DNA. So we can say that even if you do not know who your Ancestors are, they have not lost connection to you.

One concept we find today among people working with the Ancestral Spirit is known as the *Living River of Blood*. A way of understanding this idea is to think of it as an interfacing stream of energy that circulates. It flows from the Ancestors to the Living and back again. Another way to imagine this is similar to the relationship between a piece of

Living River of Blood

electrical equipment (the body) and the plug (the Ancestors). They all function together through the flow of electricity (the Living River of Blood).

We say that the Living River of Blood flows from generation to generation. However, as we shall see later in this book, there is no past, present, or future; time is a circle and not a straight line. We will set that aside for now, and look further into the concept of the River itself within the teachings presented here.

In a mystical sense, the River is where the Ancestors move to meet us. It is not their realm but is instead a conveyance we envision as a river. It is through the bloodline concept that we envision the River of Blood, the bond of lineage that literally flows through our veins just as it once did in the bodies of our Ancestors. We reach down into the blood of the "past," and our Ancestors reach up to the blood-bearers in the "present."

A very ancient model for meeting the Dead was the place of the crossroads. The center of the crossroads was considered to be a liminal area, the mystical "in-between" concept of ancient magical thinking. In such places spirits hid, and a passage into the Otherworld could be found. A related belief, in terms of place, held that spirits of the Dead can become spirits of the land, transformed into *genius loci*. The Dead could go on to an honored place among the Ancestors. The crossroads served as a gate of both entrance and exit.

There are two forms of crossroads used by our Ancestors. In Southern Europe the crossroads was the place where three roads met and formed a "Y" shape. In Northern Europe it was where four roads met in the shape of an "X" (or an equilateral cross). The southern crossroads speaks of the road traveled that leads to a change or a choice in direction. The northern one is often linked to the four directions of north, east, south, and west. In this light it is about alignments to Otherworld forces. In both the southern and northern crossroads the core matter is about the center point where the roads join together. The center is not one of the joining roads; it lays in-between. A road that is not a road, and a path that is not a path, is where magic overrides reasoning. Here it is noteworthy to take into account these words attributed to Paracelsus, a 16th-century occultist: "Magic has power to experience and fathom things which are inaccessible to human reason. For magic is a great secret wisdom, just as reason is a great public folly."

Scholar Albert Grenier, in his book *The Roman Spirit*, mentions the crossroads as a gathering place for vagabonds. This classification in ancient times included magicians, witches, and others rejected by the so-called learned class (officials and academicians). Grenier states that the vagabonds collect at the crossroads where they set an altar and celebrate as best they can, referring to themselves as The College of the Crossroads. What this means is that in ancient times the authorities issued documents known as collegia, which sanctioned a religious group and acknowledged it as being legitimate. In order to receive this document there was a requirement to demonstrate the financial means to maintain a temple and its priests/priestesses. Anyone unable to do this but still worshipping as he or she pleased was labeled by the authorities as practicing illicit religion. In defiance the vagabonds granted themselves validity and formed the *collegia compitales*—the College of the Crossroads.

Scholar Richard Gordon, in his essay "Imagining Greek and Roman Magic," adds more clarity to the views of the dominating class in terms of illicit religion. Gordon states that the "educated elite" looked down upon those not considered to be part of mainstream beliefs and practices—the Collective Civic. Non-civic rites, beliefs, and practices were considered to be nothing more than mumbo-jumbo. The view of authorities and academicians stood firmly planted in the position that valid religion is a collective matter within society; legitimate religious authority is confined to that collectivity. Something of this attitude continues into modern times. I believe this is partly the reason why folklorists were not taken seriously by historians over the past century or more. The former view folklore as unwritten history; the latter view it as fantasy. Sicilian folklorist Giuseppe Pitre was an advocate of there being two histories—that of the dominators and that of the dominated. He felt that the latter must not be confused with the former, and it was vital to save the memories of the dominated people, which conflicted with the memories of the dominators.

It is within folklore that many of the beliefs held by our Ancestors have taken refuge. The rich folklore associated with crossroads connects us with very old views, magical thinking, and religious elements. As previously noted, the Dead were associated with the crossroads. Those who had not found release from the mortal world gathered there under the care of the goddess Hecate. This idea evolved into tales of a goddess leading a train of souls across great distances on the earth (a popular theme in the Middle Ages). In some tales they travel across the sky or journey over spirit roads.

Spirit roads appear in some of the oldest stories about the Dead. Author Paul Devereux, in his article "Where the Leylines Led," writes that the lore regarding spirit roads is deep-rooted and stretches from the Eurasian landmass all the way to Ireland. The underlying belief here is that spirits move through the physical landscape along special routes. These routes are straight roads and have been known by many names such as faery paths, leylines, corpse roads, and churchway paths (to name a few).

The old faery paths linked old circular earthworks together dating from the Iron Age. These were called faery forts. So strong was the belief in faery roads that a taboo rose warning people not to block these paths by building anything on them. To do so was believed to incur the wraith of the faery folk.

One belief is that the old straight tracks allowed spirits to easily move about in the night. Winding roads confused these travelers or in some cases even blocked their passage. This idea is linked to the crossroads in the belief that dividing roads confounded the Dead (and other spirits). This caused them to become bound to the crossroads, which made the crossroads ideal for spirit contact. An unpleasant tradition came into place in the practice of burying hanged criminals at a crossroad. This was done in the belief that their souls were trapped and could not return to towns or villages seeking retaliation. Our Ancestors did not fear death as much as they feared the Dead.

It is very likely that honoring the Dead/venerating the Ancestors originated from a desire to keep peace between them and the Living. Underlying this is the need and desire to keep the Dead "in the family" and therefore still in alliance. It was, perhaps, a means of "taming" the otherwise "wild" spirits of the Dead. Here the sacredness of hearth and home continued to embrace the Dead. This in turn ensured "good spirits" who wanted to aid and guard the Living. Since these spirits were in the next world, they could be called upon to directly make contact with even the gods.

The idea eventually formed that only a veil separated the Living and the Dead. There were different realms, different types of consciousness. This was true even in the world of the Living; the waking state beneath the sun was very different from the dreaming state beneath the moon. The dream state suggested that some part of the Living passed into a world very different from the everyday world. If this was not the realm of the Dead, where was it and what part of us went there? One answer is found in the very old belief in a spirit double.

Among the clearer examples of the spirit double is the old Scandinavian belief. The general idea is that humans are comprised of three mystical spirit forms, which are the Fylgja, Hugr, and Hamr. The Fylgja is a guardian that watches over the person and looks to its overall well-being. It stays in the proximity of the person it guards.

The Hugr is a spirit that animates or gives force to the Material Body. This spirit can leave the body while the person is sleeping, and it is capable of working to manifest something desired by that person. The last of the spirits is called Hamr, and is intimately connected to the flesh body. Its quality is an energy that determines the outer form of the body it inhabits. Like the Hugr, it can leave the body and perform tasks. These are most often accomplished by the Hamr in some type of animal form.

What we are seeing in this Scandinavian system is a belief that consciousness is not entirely dependent upon a material vessel that contains it. The life force is sentient and can project from the body in this world and remain on this side of death as it desires. It can also leave the body and the world of the Living when physical death takes place. This old belief seems rooted in the concept of the soul as immortal.

In the old Hawaiian system we find striking parallels to the Scandinavian views. This is not too surprising since the Scandinavians were among the last of Europe's Pagans to fall to Christian cultural destruction against the Pagan World in an effort to convert people. In Hawaii, the native religion was already in a stage of decay when the Missionaries arrived circa 1820. Therefore, relatively little dismantling of pre-Christian ways had to be done in Hawaii, and the Missionaries focused largely on "civilizing" the native population to conform to European culture. This seemingly halfhearted effort helped protect the old ways from being erased or completely buried by the agents of Christianity in Hawaii. In both Scandinavia and Hawaii we can look at less distorted forms of Pagan beliefs than in those areas of the world that fell to Christianity centuries earlier. There is certainly less debris and fewer structures built over Paganism in these lands to obstruct our view as we explore.

The mystical or inner tradition of Hawaii lived on among individuals known as Kahuna, the shaman-like practitioner of a system called Huna. As in the Scandinavian view, the Kahuna taught that humans are comprised of three inner spirits. These are known as Unihipilli, Uhane, and Aumakua. Unihipilli forms the flesh body, and in Scandinavian beliefs we noted that Hamr determines the outer form of the human body.

Uhane is Human Consciousness hosted by Unihipilli, and both are sentient. Uhane seems to match up with Hugr, the animating spirit (at least if we look at Human Consciousness as directing the body as a vehicle). Next is Aumakua, the higher self that tends to the Unihipilli (the lower self) and also to Uhane. This seems to fit with the idea of Fylgja as the guardian and overseer. It is noteworthy that in the Scandinavian view only Fylgja is immortal, not vanishing with the others when death occurs. It is said to never die out within a family, and is therefore always connected to the Ancestors.

Because death eliminates form, the Living are charged with the task of continuing the human race. To that end we forge "the long chain" of Ancestors. The dead in turn become Ancestors, some of them return to live once again within family lines. The importance of lineage is connected to themes of Ancestral land. This in turn is tied to themes of kingship and the well-being of the land.

Many ancient tales such as that of the Arthurian legends bring us ideas about the power of the land. Here we see the strong human connection to the Enchanted World and how spirit forces work through human vessels. The idea of Excalibur, the sword in the stone, and the virtue it takes to withdraw it speak to us about the vital essence of the inner being. In the related tale of Merlin we find the importance of lineage through the bloodline of Pendragon.

The Pendragon lineage as it pertains to Ancestral themes is tied to the concept of royal blood. In the mystical tale this royal blood joins with tales of how Otherworld forces work with (and sometimes through) human lines. This generational spirit becomes tied to a quest and is selected to accomplish something of great importance to both realms—that of humankind and spiritkind alike.

Each Ancestral line has its chosen or appointed task to fulfill. Each generation sends forth its champions to serve that goal. Within these agents are the inner selves, the spirit doubles, and all the components that aid the Sacred Quest. We are all the "Once and Future King" for we have traveled across the ages in many lifetimes; we arrive in the present as the appointed stewards of our royal bloodlines. The star-blessed sword of our lineage awaits the hand that will draw it out from the stone. Sometimes that stone is deep in the sea of memory, is shadowed by towering monuments, or hidden in the faery thicket. At such times we must call to our Ancestors and lead an army of light.

CHAPTER 3

The Long Winding Road

Not long ago I watched a TV episode of *Bizarre Foods* in which the host (Andrew Zimmern) visited a tribe of Kalahari Bushmen in Botswana who reportedly live as humans did twenty thousand years ago.[1] During the filming, Zimmern attended a ritual designed to call the Ancestors. The rite was directed by a Kalahari shaman, and it involved attaining altered states of consciousness. The goal of this particular ritual was to summon the Ancestors for the purpose of healing.

As the ritual proceeded, Zimmern commented that he is a 21st-century man losing all familiar points of reference. He goes on to say that he is slipping farther away from the world as he knows it. Near the end of the rite the shaman approaches Zimmern and places a hand on his chest. Zimmern comments that something happened in that moment that he never before experienced. He goes on to say that for a moment he was in another place. Zimmern becomes emotional and starts to cry, stating that he does not understand why any of this is happening to him. In his astonishment, Zimmern remarks that he felt his life was a book of photos and someone had just spun the pages. He sums up the entire experience as something very personal that he cannot explain.

When the TV show ended, I said to myself that this man came to the crossroads where past and present generations

---

1   "Bizarre Kalahari," *Bizarre Foods, Fourth Season,* The Travel Channel, May 3, 2011, directed by Chris Marino.

meet. He clearly did not know it, but what he felt was renewal; he rejoined the Living link that flows from one generation to the next. It is noteworthy that he shed tears. In the ancient Mediterranean a belief once existed that tears entered the soil and filled a river in the Underworld. The Dead quenched their thirst in its waters, and having done so, the Dead then remembered life. Once life was remembered, the Dead desired to return once again. In this light, Zimmern may well have shared this ancient drink with those who came before him. If so, he was no longer a 21st-century man lost in time. He was instead a 21st-century man companioned by all who had come before him.

I feel it is a tragic mistake for humans to believe they exist only in the here and now. This mindset cuts us off from the *living current* that moves through time and in which all time periods flow together as one. One mystical belief calls this the Living River of Blood (a concept we encountered in a previous chapter). Without it we are left to feel alone in time and space. We simply live our lives in service to the needs of the bodies we inhabit. We die never knowing the power of the lineage we possessed in life.

Earlier in this book we noted that people often wonder whether there is a purpose in life. They ask: Why are we here? Is there an intentional reason for us to be alive here and now? Before we can understand and appreciate who we are, we must look back upon who we were in existence. This is a long and fascinating journey. It is your story.

Science tells us that particles in our bodies originally came from the stars. In other words, we animate bodies made of stardust. In a sense this means that our most distant Ancestor is the starry outer space seen in the night sky. We are descended from the stars. Our second oldest Ancestor is the earth upon which we live. In this light our nature is both celestial and terrestrial. Perhaps this seed of thought grew in the minds of our human Ancestors and became the concept of a soul within a flesh body.

Our distant Ancestors believed in "the Spirit of the Land" as something sentient in nature. It taught humans and guided them. This relationship is at the core of the idea of sacred places. In other words, the Spirit of the Land was sensed with more intensity at various specific places. Our Ancestors marked them with stones to alert people to their precise location. There are many ancient "standing stone" sites that can be thought of in this way.

Whether intentional or circumstantial, the ancient sites draw us back to our Ancestors. The stone structures influence us to think of the people who came before our time. In this light the sites are a living catalyst and an interfacing tool drawing us into the past. It is interesting to note that when people enter a sacred site, one of the first things they do is touch the stones with their hands. This is connection and it is primal. I think of this as a means of "uploading" what is stored within the stones. To me it is as though these stones recorded and archived all that was performed by humans who gathered at such sites. The songs, the prayers, the invocations, and the drumming vibrations of hands and feet upon the earth are all remembered within stone.

Who and Where Are the Ancestors?

The question as to who the Ancestors are is easily answered. They are those who came before us. They passed their knowledge, experience, and wisdom on to future generations. Collectively we call them the Ancestral Spirit. The question as to where they are is not so easily explained. In this section we will explore this theme in our search for understanding.

Humans tend to think of time as linear, and therefore we assign time to past, present, and future. This mode of thinking causes us to believe that "now" is the only reality; the past is gone and the future is yet to come. This vision is not unlike hiking up a mountain and thinking that the flat land behind us no longer exists, and what lies beyond the mountaintop is not already there until we see it.

From a metaphysical perspective the so-called past, present, and future all exist at once. Just as we can change the present, we can also change the past and the future. It is a difficult concept to fully comprehend. However, as we will see in the course of this book, one of the reasons we experience the present is to reconcile the past and recreate a balanced future. Without this concept the present can appear to be nothing more than a chance experience without much meaning. It can be reduced to just tending to your needs in the moment because you are here, and this exercise continues until you die. From a metaphysical point of view, that seems to be a waste of time within an endless Universe filled with limitless possibilities.

Our distant Ancestors tried to find reason and purpose in life. From this seeking came forth myths and legends intended to provide origins and explanations. This went hand in hand with religious beliefs and concepts. One culturally widespread tenet involved the practice of Ancestor veneration. At the core this seems connected to the ancient belief that the Dead influenced the Living. Keeping the Dead happy maintained peace; this in turn assured well-being for the Living in the future. This involved leaving offerings for the Dead, usually at a shrine or at a crossroads. In this

Ancestors among us)

light we can say that our Ancestors believed the Dead were among us or could come and go within the world of the Living.

In some ancient cultures the Dead were believed to dwell in an Underworld, with the gods or in a mystical realm. The latter was often envisioned as a secret island, or in some cases the Dead dwelled in the Faery Realm. Entrances to and from these abodes were depicted as doorways, tree hollows, misty lakes, caves, wells, or bridges. This indicates the belief of an Afterlife and a place to which the Dead traveled after leaving the world of the Living.

In some of the oldest lore concerning the Dead, they pass into a tree to await rebirth. This is connected to an ancient belief that the Dead dwell on the moon and are afterwards reborn through trees on the earth. From this depiction one can envision that the branches of trees are bridges to the Moon Realm upon which the Dead cross in their journey. This may have been one of the reasons why our Ancestors venerated trees.

In a meditation with the Greenwood Realm, I asked the question: What happens when I die? Through the "inner voice," the reply came from the Forest: "It is simple. When you die I will breathe you in, hold you for a moment, and then breathe you back into life." I found power in this imagery, and it all seemed to make sense. I am part of the cycle of life on Earth as long as I remain in the Wheel of Rebirth. In other words, as long as the soul has need of another lifetime in the Material Realm. The process of reincarnation is connected to the natural order and the cycle of things upon the earth.

One night I was talking with a friend of mine who I regard as very connected to the Otherworld or Spirit World. We discussed death and the Dead, and the conversation turned to the question: Where are the Dead? My friend remarked that the Dead are within us, within our bodies. They reside in the "River of Blood" that flows in our bodies as it once did in their flesh bodies. This river has flowed through time unbroken and unending since the first humans. The beating hearts of all your Ancestors kept this in motion and passed it on to you. Your DNA is a beacon, and is the vessel through which the flowing blood continues on through time. As long as it does, so too do the Ancestors.

One stumbling block for many people is the concept of reincarnation. This raises the question: If we are reborn, how can anyone communicate with who we once were? This is not an unreasonable question. What does happen to who we once were? One metaphysical explanation involves the concept of the "quintessence" of the soul.

The Quintessence

For the purposes of this section the soul is considered to be created by Divine Consciousness or through some Divine process. Through this the soul acquires a form in which its own sentient consciousness is housed. This Soul Body is perceived as one of energy or light. In mystical thought it is envisioned as a flame, spark, or emanation passed from the Source of All Things into souls, which then become self-aware beings. Souls are, in essence, the offspring of that which created the Universe. You are one of them. Let us look at one model showing the mystical process.

Metaphysical philosophy envisions that four elemental energies exist through which creation takes place when they join together. These elements are called Earth, Air, Fire, and Water. In ancient thought we find the idea of a fifth element, which is called the quintessence. From an alchemical perspective this is what is created when forces condense into oneness. In the case of the Four Elements, the quintessence arises when something merges with the four elemental natures.

The soul in its natural environment has an Energy Body. It contains all the imprints from all the lives it experienced through reincarnation. An easy way to think of this is as follows. At one time in your life you were a certain age within the decades of child, teen, and adult. For example, you can think back on being a teenager. This memory can evoke how you felt at the time, or simply allow you to recall yourself at that time in your life. However, you are no longer that teenager; you are no longer that person. You have simply retained the experience, and it has been added to all that you are right now. In this same way the soul retains and remembers all its lifetime experiences through the people it once animated. It is, however, none of the people from those past lives. It is the accumulation of them all, and so we can say it is the quintessence of distilled lifetimes. In this light, you are the quintessence of your current lifetime experiences.

In the spiritual evolution of the soul it is important to differentiate lifetime experiences gained through individual personalities. What this means is that each lifetime is experienced through a *persona* that is mentored by the soul. The two share consciousness while in the flesh body. This is much like an actor playing a specific role. While in that role the actor becomes and *is* that character. An actor cannot take that character into a new and unrelated movie. He or she must become the different character needed for the next movie production. All of this hones the skills, knowledge, and presence of the actor.

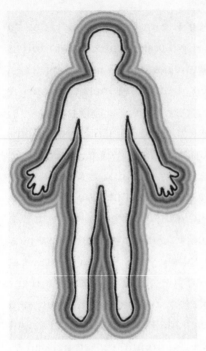

One metaphysical model for the soul incorporates the concept of five *bodies* that form with the soul in each lifetime. Only one of the bodies is of a material nature; the others are etheric or energetic fields. They form bands of energy that outline the central Material Body. Beginning from the outermost band inward, we can label them Soul, Spirit, Aura, Astral, and Material. The soul encloses them all in its being.

The image shows the material form (or flesh body) enclosed within four bands of etheric bodies. Together they establish five shared forms that generate the "quintessence of being" in its totality. The quintessence emanates from the integration of these bodies with the soul.

The Material Body is the dense material form. It is the last phase of manifestation and serves as means for the soul to remain within the Material Realm. Without this housing, the soul would withdraw through attraction back to a realm suited to its non-material nature (like attracts like). The flesh body is not only an anchor; it is also a beacon for the Ancestral Spirit. Lineage and communication are never lost.

The Astral Body is an ether-like image of the material form. It is a metaphysical principle that material objects first begin as astral images of them, which then condense into material forms of the astral likeness. While an Astral Body is attached to a Material Body, it is used to carry consciousness into the Dream Realm or into Astral Realms. The Astral Body has all the senses of the physical form, which is why we see, hear, feel, and speak in dreams (and elsewhere).

The Aura Body is the energy pattern reflecting the "state of being" of the personality worn by the soul. Colors indicating the spiritual vibration of the personality emanate within the aura of the individual. From a metaphysical perspective, the lighter the color, the higher the spiritual vibration. The energy of the aura is a contributing factor in our "first impression" of a person. You have probably met someone for the first time and almost instantly liked or disliked the person. Positive or negative feelings about someone are often due to sensing the auric energy around him or her. In this light it is important to note that the aura usually indicates temporary states of being. This changes along with events and conditions in the person's life, and therefore the aura shifts and transforms from day to day. In accord, the colors within an aura change as well, although there is always a background wash of color to the aura that is the general nature of the persona.

The Spirit Body holds the consciousness of the individual worn and animated by the soul. It is sentient and separate on its own from the soul. It is you as the actor portrayed by you the soul. In this light your life is the movie throughout which your soul portrays and projects the role of the character cast in the film. When someone says that another person is such a beautiful spirit, they are talking about what they sense emanating from the Spirit Body. This body survives the initial death experience of the flesh, unlike the Astral Body which quickly dissolves back into the Astral Realm. Further information on the Spirit Body is found in the section on Death and the Dead.

The soul is the original and true vessel of your being. It is who you truly are, and is most recognizable when not acting the role of a character in any given lifetime. It is important to know that you are not the personality in this lifetime. The person on your ID card is not you. You are greater than this finite manifestation, greater than what stands before you in the mirror. You are eternal, but what you see in the mirror is fleeting.

The metaphysical teaching here is that the soul descends into reincarnation through a process. This involves passing through several energetic fields that are called realms, but in effect they are emanations of a different frequency. These energy fields add their unique and specific energy imprint to the Soul Body as it moves through each one. From a mystical perspective, the soul descends from the Stellar Realm that is its natural environment. It then passes through the Solar Realm where it is imprinted with an astrological design and pattern. This appears as the Natal Chart and Sun Sign. In essence this is a type of map to aid the soul in any given lifetime. It defines the strengths and the challenges for the personality, and it offers insights into the experiences that are drawn to it in each lifetime.

Next in order, the soul passes through what is called the Lunar Realm. Here the Earth Plane body for the soul is envisioned in accord with the vibrations that added to the soul from the stellar and solar influences. The sensitive and receptive nature of the astral substance (the Lunar nature) reacts and creates an energy form that will condense and become the intended physical body. I say "intended" because material things and situations can alter a growing fetus once conception manifests. One metaphysical belief is that the soul chooses a human bloodline, which has its own traits carried in the DNA. This being foreknowledge, the Astral Body allows for this factor when envisioning the Material Body. Later in this book we will look at how communication between the Ancestors and the soul initiates the entire process.

The final descent into reincarnation requires a Material Body. There are several metaphysical theories as to how this process works. I favor the concept that souls are drawn into a vortex that is created by the energy of sexual intercourse. The soul passes into this vortex portal, and if conception takes place, the soul is bound within the womb gate. This concept has two different schools of thought. One view is that the soul becomes attached to the expectant mother's aura and is later drawn into the infant when it takes its first breath of air. The other view is that the soul enters the fetus at the moment of conception.

With the birth of the infant the soul is now rooted in the Material Realm. It will gradually integrate into the Material Body and slowly relinquish its identity to the host, who will then emerge as the persona or personality of the living individual. One school of metaphysical thought holds that this process takes seven days. This is the same amount of time it takes the soul to disengage its connection to the Material Body following the material death experience. During this period the personality is free to visit loved ones, friends, and other people still among the Living.

During a material lifetime the persona experiences material life and the soul integrates the experience into its own core being. Although each lifetime offers the soul a series of lessons to aid its evolution, the one common acquisition is compassion. However, the soul does not enter into reincarnation solely for its own advancement.

According to one metaphysical school of thought the soul serves as a transmitter back to the Divine Consciousness.

This allows the Source of All Things to view its creation from all possible angles. Each persona collects data through its experience of material existence, which is then received by Divine Consciousness through the soul's direct connection to its consciousness. You can think of this as being similar to how we obtain information through the senses of our flesh body. Individual cells in the Material Body constantly transmit to the brain, and from these transmissions a person is informed about their condition and the world around them. He or she then adjusts as needed or desired. In this light, souls can be regarded as cells in the mind of the Source of All Things. In some religions we find the idea that "God" is all-knowing. Perhaps each sentient being is part of that knowing through its communication with the Source of All Things.

At some point in material existence the flesh body will die. This disconnects the soul and the persona. The Astral Body and the aura quickly dissolve because they no longer receive energy from the material form. The Spirit Body preserves the persona. One belief is that the Spirit Body is eventually integrated into the Ancestral Spirit, and we can liken this to what is called the "hive mind." We see an example of this in beehives where a single bee functions with others as one consciousness—the Group Mind.

When all the energy bodies that were once attached to the soul are shed, the soul returns to full self-awareness (now that is it no longer distracted with the multiple attachments that drew upon it). This is the moment of liberation because nothing is now keeping the soul bound to the Material Plane of existence. At this moment the soul awakens from the dream of life, rises, and returns back home again to its natural environment. It has reclaimed its individual identity from the host.

The disembodied persona is ultimately drawn into the collective of the Ancestral Spirit where it joins others of its DNA lineage. In some cases, such as a traumatic death, the persona may remain for a period of time on the Earth Plane in its Spirit Body. This is a conscious haunting in which the persona can interact with the Living. It is a difficult concept to understand that the persona is a shared consciousness with the soul, and that the soul is the consciousness that can continue to experience beyond its former life as that specific persona. It may help to understand that the persona is not reincarnated; the soul is reincarnated. The persona remains the being it was in life, and dwells with its Ancestors as one of their own. There it grows in the rich collective wisdom of the Ancestral Spirit and evolves to become a guardian and guide to humans in other lifetimes.

Past Life Memories

In some mystical traditions of the past we find that initiates were trained to recall previous lifetimes. This was done in part to take away the fear of death through discovering that life and death are a cycle. They are not finite, they are cyclical. Most people do not recall their past lives unless they work to discover them. This state appears to be natural. Although past lives are intriguing, is there any reason other than curiosity to recall them?

It is one metaphysical concept that a past life trauma is carried over into the next lifetime if it was not resolved by the soul. This is not unlike the experience of trauma in any current life, and many people seek counseling to help them resolve it. Violence, abuse, and oppression in any decade of our life can affect our current mental and emotional health. Counseling is a way of looking at our past, understanding how it affects us now, and discovering ways to resolve it so we can be liberated from this influence.

Most people do not require counseling, and in this same way most people have not had past lives that left any trauma significant enough to carry over into another lifetime. In this light the recollection of past lives is not required nor will its memory necessarily aid the work of the soul in its current material life. We are, however, left with the problem of our Ancestors who lived lives of personal trauma, or who caused serious trauma to others.

Our distant Ancestors understood that the living generation is never cut off from the past generation. The influence is always present and always active. In an old movie titled *The Emerald Forest* there is an important scene that connects with the Ancestral Spirit. The movie is based on a true story of a South American tribe living naturally within the forest. This makes the scene all that more important to our understanding because in living naturally the tribe is still an active part of the living roots. They have not been "robbed of the magic" by the distractions of modern life.

In one part of the movie we find the tribe performing a ceremony for their recent dead. The bodies are cremated and the remains are ground in a stone mortar and pestle-style implement. A large gourd (decorated to resemble a pregnant woman) is then produced. It contains some of the ashes of all of the Ancestors of the tribe. The chief states that this goes back to the first Ancestor. A portion of the ashes of the newly cremated are added to the gourd and mixed in by hand. The chief then scoops up some of the mixed ash and adds it to a drinking gourd filled with water. This is passed around to each tribe member and each one drinks from the gourd. This practice can be shocking and repulsive to the average person in modern society. At the core modern people have lost their connection to the Ancestral Spirit; therefore intimate contact with it is something alien.

In a meditation I was introduced to the theme of modern burial practices of preservation. Unlike the majority of our Ancestors, today the body is preserved and sealed in a coffin that is designed to survive the ages. It does not become absorbed into the earth like the bare wood coffins of past centuries. From a mystical perspective it does not become embraced by the Spirit of the Land, at least not in the intended organic sense. In this light it appears that modern burial practices may interfere with, or delay, the natural process through which each generation is connected together. It may be that such practices create a weak signal and make it difficult to interface directly with the Ancestral Spirit. In my meditation a thought arose that in modern culture the religious or spiritual focus is upon the heaven worlds, the celestial. Modern humans have disconnected from the terrestrial connection known to our Ancestors. Perhaps the modern view of the earth as nothing but a resource to be plundered stems from this detachment that favors a heaven world versus the one of our Ancestors.

In one teaching, the Ancestors are said to have a vested interest in the living generation. The Dead want to be remembered, and the living generation sustains them energetically when they are honored and venerated. In another chapter you will find rituals, customs, and ceremonies to keep and strengthen ties with your lineage.

Earlier in this chapter I mentioned the idea of the Living River of Blood that flows through each generation. The Ancestors communicate to us from the cellular level of our bodies. You carry this connection within your body, and your

DNA is the bridge erected by your Ancestors. You stand on one side of it as the steward of your entire lineage. You are the current keeper of the River of Blood that flows from all who came before you.

The River of Blood Through Time

In my previous book *The Cauldron of Memory*, I explored the idea of what is passed to us within our DNA. We know, of course, that in the DNA of our parents we receive the instructions on how to build us. This is the material reality. The metaphysical perspective is that we also receive the memories or the distilled experiences of our Ancestors. In this light we find one explanation for such things as child prodigies, and for phobias that have no basis in current experiences (as well as personal mannerisms that were previously those of someone departed).

Our DNA possesses particles and energy, which is a relationship not unlike that of the terrestrial and celestial. This was passed to us from the DNA that existed in the bodies of our parents, which contained the DNA passed to them by their parents. This DNA chain goes back to the very beginning. As mentioned earlier in this book, you exist as a person because each of your Ancestors in your direct lineage lived long enough to reproduce. You come from an ancient unbroken chain that survived the ages.

In some systems of metaphysics the phrase Living River of Blood is used in reference to the concept of the continuing Ancestral presence. The basic idea is that within our cellular makeup is an interfacing or meeting point between us and our direct Ancestors. As mentioned earlier the DNA particles and the biological energies are beacons for the Ancestral spirit, and we previously touched on the idea of morphogenetic fields.

Another aspect is known as morphic resonance, a principle championed by biologist Rupert Sheldrake.

Morphic resonance is a process whereby inherited memories are passed. Sheldrake points out that memory need not be "coded in genes" but is conveyed through resonance from previous members of the same species. In this light each individual inherits a collective memory. Morphic fields can also influence individuals bathed in the energetic current. Here we begin to catch a glimpse of how the "voices" of the Ancestors are not echoes through time; they are active communication.

One metaphysical tenet is "as above, so below," meaning that the material and non-material realms share likeness. For every law or principle of physics there is a corresponding one in metaphysics. In this light we can say that group connections (and family lineages) exist on both planes. They share a morphic field and remain connected. This is one way in which we can think of the mechanics of connecting with the Ancestral Spirit, or more accurately with its collective.

We have touched on the idea of the Ancestors communicating through the River of Blood, but this begs the question as to why and how this takes place. Let us begin first with the question of why. One answer resides in a two-part concept. The idea is that some of our Ancestors require formal "redemption" or healing for lives that resulted in negative energies that delay full transition following the death experience. In this light you have returned, in part, to aid them. Additionally, bloodlines that are still working to manifest something in the world of the Living need a living agent. Both of these situations can draw a soul to enter a specific bloodline and champion the cause. Further on in this book you will find rituals you can use on behalf of your Ancestors.

The pride that people feel in their nationality, and the attraction to discover details about their Ancestors, is more about a living energetic connection than a desire to satisfy curiosity. The pull is from the roots; it is a calling to take the position of a bridge and to be a vessel that connects past and present. You are the needed synapse that can bring the Ancestral consciousness through time. It is one of the reasons why your soul currently resides within a body, which is linked to the experiences of a bloodline. Through the cellular consciousness of your DNA you can interface with your Ancestors. They are not as distant as you may think.

The Ancestral Realm

Ancient myths and legends paint various pictures of an Afterlife. Some envision heaven worlds, underworlds, great banquet halls, and so on. These depictions are subscriptions to religious beliefs that provide a specific notion regarding what happens following the physical death of an individual. One less built upon that view is that when a person dies she or he enters into the Ancestral Realm at one point. This is a dimension that maintains the individual's consciousness within a collective. To try and understand this it helps to accept that the personality in each life is released by the soul. What enters the Ancestral Realm is the persona that was worn and enlivened by the soul. The soul is you; the persona is the role you played in material life.

An associated metaphysical perspective is that when different nationalities interbreed the offspring are connected by an interlacing field. In this light there can be various lineage attachments within the Ancestral Realm. For example, a person who is part German, Scottish, and Italian is connected with those lineages through a type of morphogenetic field that networks with others in morphic resonance. We should note that the Ancestral Realm is not actually a place per se; it is a state of being symbolized by the concept of the Ancestral Spirit.

In metaphysical philosophy there are seven planes that comprise Universal existence. These are envisioned as Ultimate, Divine, Spiritual, Mental, Astral, Elemental, and Material. The Material Plane is where energy is so dense and concentrated that things appear and act as solid objects. This state of existence binds energy fields to it much like a planet holds its atmosphere. In this light we can say that the Ancestral Spirit is bound to the land or to the Spirit of the Land. This gives stronger meaning to the idea of Ancestral lands. In effect the Ancestral Spirit is indeed connected with the Spirit of the Land, and dwells in-between the Organic Memory of the Earth and the Elemental Plane. More details can be found in the chapter on Death and Rebirth.

In previous writings I have discussed the idea of the Organic Memory of the Earth. The concept is rooted in the fact that all living beings go into the soil following material death. There they decompose and become absorbed beneath the land (the exception being body preservation). The metaphysical principle is that this forms a reservoir of their experiences, the memories of all that had been. This zone is sometimes called Shadow. We can liken this to the idea in Eastern Mysticism of the Akashic Records, which is a concept that all memories are held in the bound energy field of the earth. Perhaps we are looking at spiritual and organic counterparts.

In my personal work with the Ancestral Spirit I find it most effective to connect inward. I can *feel* my Ancestors within my body, and my body is linked to the Spirit of the Land. My Ancestors seem to speak loudest at sacred sites, cemeteries, and in that state of being between dreaming and awakening. I sense the Ancestors outside of me as well as inside.

 Over time I entered into an "agreement of consciousness" with my Ancestors from which arose the vision of the Ancestral Realm as a beehive. I like this imagery for it is not unlike the ancient burial mounds of our Ancestors in which a single hole opened into the interior. Archaeologists and some anthropologists believe this was designed as a type of doorway through which the soul could exit and enter the mound (and by extension the Hidden Realm within it). Similarities exist in the lore connected to openings into a Faery mound.

Regarding the theme of a hole as the entrance and exit to the Ancestral Realm, we find a connection to serpent symbolism. Snakes disappear into burrows, which connects them to themes of the Underworld. They also shed their skins, a trait that links them to reincarnation. It is interesting to note that our DNA has a serpent-like appearance in its double helix formation.

Many cultures that practice Ancestral veneration include serpent symbolism of one type or another. In ancient Rome we find the Lare spirit, which represents the Guardian Spirit of the surviving family lineage. Ancient Roman households featured a portrait of the head of the family (as genii or begetter) flanked on each side by Lare. Beneath the images a serpent represented the Ancestral spirit depicted as moving along the foundation. All of this symbolism expressed the importance of preserving lineage. Further information about the Lare spirit is found in Appendix Two.

In ancient imagery the serpent is a symbol of health (as in the caduceus) and also a protector and preserver. The latter

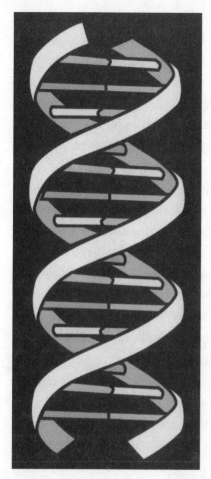

is found in the old practice of placing a snake in the grain storage bins to help prevent the supplies from being consumed by rodents. This promotes the idea of the snake being the protector and preserver of seeds, which is symbolic of aiding the Ancestral lineage.

Mythological snakes are sometimes associated with trees of which they are guardians. This theme was later changed to depict the snake as an evil character as reflected in the myth of Adam and Eve in old Hebrew culture. As mentioned in Chapter Two, ancient lore indicates a belief that humans are born from trees (and a belief that souls await rebirth in trees). It is interesting to note that the hollow of a tree was believed to be an entrance to the Faery Realm. Some commentators have linked the Faery Realm with the Land of the Dead. This is based upon the idea of old Neolithic burial mounds and their later connection to the lore of Faery mounds through which faeries and their world can be encountered.

Ancient Greek philosophers such as Plutarch wrote that the souls of the Dead reside on or in the moon. One mystical thought is that the moon collects the souls of the Dead each night as it crosses over the world of mortalkind. The light of these souls is gathered in by the moon and its brightness expands until it is full (of souls). As souls are released back into mortal bodies the light of the moon decreases until it can no longer be seen in the night sky.

We can think of the moon as symbolizing the survival of the soul. The sun, a symbol of daily life, diminishes and dies as it sets. The moon represents the survival of that worldly light (the soul) into the next phase (the night). This metaphor speaks to the mystical concept of this world and the Otherworld. The Living walk in sunlight, and the Dead walk in moonlight.

Scholar Jules Cashford, in her book *The Moon: Myth and Image*, writes that the moon has long been regarded as a portal or doorway to another realm. She goes on to refer to the moon as the door to the eternal world. Cashford remarks that the moon is beyond the phenomena of time and change, which are connected to the earthly realm. Within the realm of the moon souls are received and regenerated.

Some ancient writers refer to a mystical island of the Dead that lies in a vast sea. This "island" is the moon and the "sea" is the vast night sky. In tales of this nature souls are depicted as journeying by boat to the island. This is reminiscent of the Greek myths in which the Dead must give the ferryman a coin for passage. In this idea we can see a symbolic depiction of the soul relinquishing its material form (represented by the coin) so that it can move on to a nonmaterial realm.

In a spiritual sense, the moon can be a symbol for us of the Ancestral Realm or the light of the Ancestral Spirit itself. The changing and ever-returning display of its cycles speaks to us from another realm of the great mysteries of birth, life, death, and renewal. The Ancestral wisdom shines down upon us from the night sky. It is enlightenment in the places of darkness; we are guided and companioned by all who have gone before us. That covenant shines brightly in the night sky.

CHAPTER 4

†here and Back Again
(The Soul's Return)

There is a mystical teaching that advises the reincarnating soul to reunite with others it knew in a previous life. Different versions of it exist but the most common one reads:

> *There are three great mysteries in the life of man—love, death, and resurrection in a new body. To fulfill love you must return at the same time and place as the loved one, and you must meet and know and remember and love them again. But to be reborn you must die and be ready for a new body; to die you must be born; without love you may not be born.*

This is linked to a metaphysical concept that a soul can pick up where it left off in a specific past life. One teaching is that souls travel in groups through time. Momentum is gained through remaining in alliance with other souls who were specific people known to the soul in a past life. There is less "starting over" in this scenario, and the souls continue their work together through intentional designs and purposes. A pact with the Ancestral Spirit goes hand in hand with such returns as we will see in the pages to follow.

In terms of reincarnation there are many ideas as to its necessity or purpose. In this chapter we will explore this consideration along with various elements not often presented on the topic. One example is the question of being reborn within a specific bloodline or nationality. Is this just random, or does the soul play a part in choosing the DNA link within a flesh body?

Several years ago I had a dream in which I was dead. I waited in line with other dead people to pass through a doorway. The door was at the end of an antechamber that had many shelves along its walls. Each shelf contained a newborn infant. A spirit being within the chamber asked if anyone wanted to take a baby along when they passed through the doorway. In the dream I thought it might be comforting to hold something as I passed into the unknown that waited beyond the door. As soon as I picked up a newborn baby, the spirit grinned, snapped his fingers, and shouted "Reincarnated!"— and so I was. I had, in effect, chosen another physical form to inhabit.

This dream influenced me to look beyond all that I had previously learned about reincarnation through the decades of my studies. The idea that a soul selects its next life and its parents was always a frequent theme in books on reincarnation. The common thought is that the soul knows things about what the next material life will offer the soul's education. It also knows something about how the parents will affect the soul's experience in any given lifetime. Following the dream I began to think in terms of the DNA as a beacon. Do we choose more than what a specific life has to teach the soul? Do we also choose a genetic heritage, a lineage to which we become tied? If so, why do we make that choice?

To answer that question we need to first look at the advantages of reincarnating. One important element is how material existence impacts the consciousness as opposed to non-material reality. One way of looking at this is to compare the so-called "waking state" with the so-called "dream state" that we experience each day and night. In the waking state things are linear, connected to cause and effect, responsive in kind, and constant in nature. For example, a chair remains a chair the next day. We have to walk, drive/be driven, or fly in a machine in order to get somewhere. Gravity is constant, time is a measurement, and one action results in another. This is not the same in the consciousness of our dream state.

In dreams things change from moment to moment, and there is no reliance upon anything adhering to a linear movement. We appear in places without ever traveling to get there. Time is not a factor in the dream world, and actions can be unrelated to outcomes. You can pick up a gun to defend yourself only to discover that you are holding a watering hose and tending to a garden. Dream consciousness is all about being in the moment and going with whatever shifts take place. It is more about the message and less about the means through which that message is delivered. However, the parts of the whole are important and should not be neglected.

If we apply the idea of learning within a classroom to the concepts of the waking state and the dream state, which condition is best suited to learning something specific? The answer, of course, is the waking state. Its finite and stable nature allows us to assemble practical knowledge piece by piece. By contrast, the dream state allows us to use what we have learned about material reality within a non-material realm. When you need to do something in the dream world, you apply your knowledge of the material world. For example you might run if something is after you. You might look for something or someone in a dream that you desire to connect with. These are all material rules, and you repeatedly use them in dreams even when they are dysfunctional in that state of consciousness. No doubt you have had dreams in which the props keep changing into something else when you need them.

What this all boils down to is that souls benefit from specific experiences that are only possible in a finite reality—the waking state. The limitations of a Material Body, and the rules of a material reality, come together to provide the soul with a stable foundation upon which to build. The material world is a classroom of linear teachings and lessons. It prepares us for existence within a non-material reality that has a completely different set of rules. Abstract can only be conceived of if conventional is experienced beforehand for we define things when we know their opposites. Material reality provides the means through which we can compare, contrast, and distinguish.

One teaching is that consciousness is developed and honed through the experience of repeating cycles. Since dreams do not produce reliable repeating cycles within them for us, we turn to material reality for the needed reliable patterns. It is through the "constant" that we develop our conscious awareness of existence. Material existence, for the soul, is very much about orientations, rhythms, and impacts that cause permanent changes.

The mystic William G. Gray wrote in his book *Western Inner Workings* that "Consciousness is cyclical and advances around its center in helical manner like other rhythmic energies of our Universe." He goes on to say that we perceive things as linear in the material world (and by the way we reason) because we cannot sense the curvature of consciousness through time. He likens this to us not being able to see the curative of the earth while standing on it, even though the earth is round and spinning in outer space. Now think about this: Our Ancestors once believed the earth to be flat, and that the sun revolved around it. It was not until we fully perceived the annual repeating cycles of Nature that we became able to expand our consciousness beyond our sensory abilities. These expansions led us to learn about a reality that was previously obscured by the limitations of self-focus (or more accurately by our tiny inward spirals of consciousness). We came to understand that the earth is round and that it orbits the sun; this realization became possible because we observed the repeated cycles of the seasons, and fell into rhythm with the tides and forces of the earth.

Gray states that "souls evolve through the experience of cyclical consciousness." This speaks to the *need* for repeated lifetimes in the Material Realm. However, the soul eventually moves on to experience "lifetimes" in non-material realms as well, but we will explore that later in the book. For now we will keep our focus on the soul in a Material Body.

Our distant Ancestors left us many ancient symbols. Among the oldest and most lasting is the spiral. We can think of this as a cyclical symbol, and in that light it can be seen as a reminder that consciousness is connected to cycles. It is interesting to note that in Nature we find a significant spiral that is named the Fibonacci spiral. It is found in plants, in shell formations, and in the formation of some animal horns. It is also the shape of spirals that form weather pressure systems on the earth. In addition it is the spiral shape that galaxies take on. In mathematics the Fibonacci sequence demonstrates how things form and expand. It is noteworthy that in the Fibonacci design we have a joining of both the celestial and the terrestrial. So too is it with soul's journey in which its stellar nature joins with a material form upon the Earth Plane of existence.

The material form provides the soul with more than just a body to use in a given lifetime. Its DNA provides the history of a people with a story to tell through time. Every story is valuable even when it lies quietly in the spirit of someone who carries it silently and deeply within them. In each lifetime you get to add to that story and perhaps even to complete it and start another. Just like an actor accepts an offer to perform in a movie, show, or play, the soul chooses to enter into the story of a bloodline. The soul is drawn into a lineage that anchors it in a specific current within the Material Plane. There are many lessons to be gained and many challenges to temper the soul. There is also a flowing *river of consciousness* from the past that empowers us with knowledge and wisdom. Its fount is the Ancestral Spirit.

The metaphysical view here is that events that affected previous generations, as well as our own Ancestral bloodline, are inherited by humans. These are active currents that saturate the soul upon entry into a Material Body. We are all affected by them to varying degrees, and we are here to affect them as well. One way we can accomplish this is to unite with the cycles that our Ancestors connected with in their own time periods. These patterns are in us and they are in nature; we need only embrace them. We can do this, in part, by returning to the celebrations and acknowledgments of the things that enriched the lives of our Ancestors.

The change from a past lifestyle known to our distant Ancestors (and the adaptations to modern life) has caused humans to be dominated by linear thinking. Contemporary humans tend to think in straight lines and therefore perceive of things progressing forward in distinct stages. This mentality tends to leave things behind, and it keeps the future always as something that may or may not happen. This is contrary to the mechanism of Nature, which operates in reliable repeating cycles. For example, the Four Seasons move in a circle, not a straight line. We cannot directly perceive this anymore than our senses can directly perceive our planet as being round. Our eyes see the world as flat (but containing terrain) from horizon to horizon. But that is not the reality of the world in which we exist. Our planet is not only circular; it circles around the sun, which in turn moves with the circular spiral of the galaxy. Reality is circles within circles, wheels within wheels.

Our distant Ancestors learned about their world through recognizing the rhythms of Nature. Seasonal rites were created to mark these repeating events. Our Ancestors understood them to be important parts of something greater, a larger Whole. In time the seasonal markers took on spiritual significance as well as announcing the arrival of planting and harvesting opportunities (along with the observational migration of herds and flocks). From this genetic memory within us we possess that same Ancestral clock.

William Gray refers to the matching cycles of Nature within us, and he applies a model called the Cosmic Cross. This symbol, in part, represents the teaching that we should strive to be "intentionally conscious" with the "Cosmic Life Spirit" as it presents itself amidst the rising seasonal shifts. What this means is that there are connections in the earth's cycles to cycles within higher planes. This is reflected in the Hermetic axiom: "That which is above is as that which is below, and that which is below is as that which is above." The teaching here is that the planes of existence reflect upon each other, showing us facets of the common denominator, which is the Source of All Things, the Divine Consciousness. What we need to understand is that our bodies are linked to our Ancestors, and this is the first circle we enter. From there we expand outward to meet the Universe.

The Cosmic Cross provides us with a compass of sorts, a way of connecting with Ancestral understanding and the important mechanism our Ancestors knew very well through personal experience. It is also a primitive type of calendar, and in it we see the points of the Solstice and Equinox periods that are pivotal in the Wheel of the Year. Let us examine the symbolism of the Cosmic Cross.

Looking at the symbol, the interior lines represent the following:

The Four Cardinal Points: North, East, South, West

The Four Seasons: Spring, Sumner, Fall, Winter

The Four times of Day: Morning, Noon, Evening, Night

The Four Worlds of Mystic Thought: Stellar, Solar, Lunar, Material

Enclosing the lines we see the circle, which represents spiral consciousness and the return to ways of thinking that are not dominated by linear ones. It is a reminder that we evolve outward from the center. We begin from consciousness of the body, then move to its locality upon the earth, next to the world at large, and finally out to the cosmos. Therefore being in a body connects us to cellular consciousness, which then opens in the consciousness of our entire body. Having a body gives us spatial life awareness, and animation of the body allows us to experience the world beyond our finite location. This broadening of consciousness acclimates and orients us to see the greater solar system that our world is part of, and in doing so we can see beyond ourselves. The more we evolve the wider our realizations become, and the further in space our experience extends. This eventually leads to being released from the cycle of reincarnation because the lessons learned from material existence have been exhausted. We return home to the Community of Souls.

What's a Soul to Do?

There is more to the matter of the soul than simply being in partnership with an Ancestral lineage. A greater purpose is attached to the soul's return to the Material Realm. This realm is the most condensed concept of creation and therefore a tangible one that you can literally get your hands on. Its creation came down from the other planes of existence (much like steam condenses into water). We are, in a sense, experiencing the end product. However, we are not the purchasers; we are the test group for the manufacturer.

This view centers on the concept that the soul serves as a transmitter to and a receiver from Divine Consciousness. In this light the soul conveys to Divine Consciousness its experiences, perceptions, and reactions within the Material Plane. Through this, Divinity assesses its creation and makes adjustments (not always in favorable ways to humankind).

Informing Divinity is a great responsibility, and it requires careful and thoughtful discernment. In metaphysics there is a saying that "thoughts are things." What this means is that our minds create realities in which we operate, and those realities affect other people as well. We are all causing ripples, and those ripples go much further than most people might think.

In material existence the soul is encumbered with the human condition. It is, in effect, distracted and can be overloaded by sensory input. This limits the full focus of the soul's consciousness. There are methods to help alleviate this situation such as meditation, self-discipline exercises, and spiritual pursuits. The goal is to create a state of consciousness that is not reactive, but is instead discerning in positive ways. In this manner we can become more effective receivers and transmitters to Divine Consciousness. This requires turning off our personal filters and suspending our preconceived notions in the moment. It is not an easy task but it is quite worthy of attainment (for our own good as well as the greater good).

If we envision our thoughts as energy forms, what kind of energy is most beneficial to generate? What do our thoughts and feelings communicate to others and to the Universe about our state of being? The Universe is, in effect, listening to us. What you spend most of your time believing or disbelieving becomes your reality. The Universe matches your energy with like kind. If you spend time and energy thinking of gain, then the Universe adds to it. On the other hand if you spend time and energy thinking of lack, then the Universe pours that into your life as well. It does not reason or think in human ways or with human judgment; it simply responds to energy in like kind. Try not to think of this as reward or punishment because it is not. Think of it as "cause and effect" because that is what it really is all about. All this being said, it should be noted that the free will of other people inserted into our lives can impact what we work to create and manifest. This can be in undermining ways as well as in positive ways. For example someone can withhold or deny you money you are due just as someone can loan you money you don't have.

In being transmitters and receivers, we are like brain cells in the mind of the Divine. This idea was touched upon earlier but there is more to the concept. We not only inform the Source of All Things, we can become its means of changing the status quo. It may well be that we are the only beings on Earth that consciously set about accomplishing such a task. This is a great responsibility. It requires careful expansive thought and vision.

Affecting material existence cannot be left in the hands of those who see the earth (and other planets) as a resource that can be plundered for financial profit. If you think of bloodlines, then it will not surprise you to know that certain ones control a great deal of wealth. This wealth weighs heavy on the backs of those who are not part of its lineage or heritage. If we envision a world in which greed does not pay and in which fairness and equality are the norms, we can focus our energy and send waves towards manifestation. The alternative is to be passive and allow others to create the world and the reality in which we live. We have a choice even though there are people who do not want us to know or experience that reality.

One metaphysical concept we touched on earlier is that souls travel in groups and reincarnate in number. They can and do come into specific time periods for a reason. In our own century the souls of the Old World and the Old Ways are returning and creating a difference. This entry is a balance shift; it is a spiritual reaction to centuries of being constrained and fitted with blinders by dominating religions and organizations. The Neo-Pagan movement is but one example of this shift, and in it we are seeing a return to pre-Christian religions as well as a membership increase in non-Christian ones. Our Ancestors have a vested interest in the world of the Living, and they are calling for souls who are the allies sharing the vision for healing and protecting our planet, our world. Other souls long for the end of the world, a destruction that leads to a realm of paradise set aside exclusively for them. The Universe is listening and counting votes.

Incarnate: The Triformis Nature

The number three represents an active principle whereas the number two represents balance as in a state of stasis. The principle of "three" releases the finite and liberates expansion. This is one of the meanings of the term "triformis" and we see it as a symbol that is well-known to our Ancestors.

The triformis nature is often regarded as a symbol for transformation. It works in joining the soul to material form, and then releasing it back into non-material existence. However it also plays a role during each physical lifetime. We experience this through the principles of what is known in metaphysics as *space*, *time*, and *event*—in other words, where we are, when we are, and our perception of what is happening where the two intersect in our lives. Let us examine each element.

The simple definition of space is the point or place at which you are conscious. It is where you are and where you can be found. However, the greater purpose of spatial awareness is orientation. As humans on the earth we orient to directions such as north, east, south, west, above, below, and in-between. These are agreements of consciousness shared by humans. These things do not actually exist outside of our perspective. For example in outer space there are no directions, no above or below. So we agree as humans that directions exist and we adhere to them in our navigation. The same is true of our spiritual landscapes during our explorations (while tied to material existence). It is our sense of space that allows us to map a connection to our Ancestors (we as *here*, and they as *there*).

Next in triformis order is time. On the surface time is the awareness of "now" and the projection backward to the "past" and forward to the "future." It is another agreement of consciousness shared by humans for points of reference. The soul does not relate to the concept of past and future but is instead centered in now. The personality worn by the soul in each lifetime perceives existence as linear: past, present, future. For metaphysical purposes time is the awareness of cycles that present themselves. The Four Seasons, for example, are catalysts to our awareness of the parts that make up the whole (the Year). Time is the means by which we interface with space. This allows action when joined with the concept of direction (we can go there and meet here). This principle can be seen in marking out a site with a stone circle (space) and then treading (time) to cardinal points within the structure.

The final aspect of triformis is what we call event. Simply understood, events are the things that happen to us or the things we engage in. Metaphysically speaking, events are moments of change (most of them permanent). Events affect our experience of time and space. Some events are random occurrences while others are directed to us. An auto accident, for example, can change everything in your life in one single moment. The willful act of another human being can do the same. It is important to understand that these things offer us reactions to them. The "why" of it pales in connection to the way we respond and deal with the matter. One example I use in classes is the alligator in the swimming pool scenario. Most people in this position will first fixate on why there is an alligator in the pool, and how it got there to begin with. This is all irrelevant to the situation because the setting calls for a reaction, which is getting the alligator out of the swimming pool. Our reactions shape us, and in them we have opportunities to embrace a spiritual emanation. It is as William Gray wrote about space, time, and event:

> *The guiding principle behind them all is to make your-self intentionally conscious of the Cosmic Life Spirit in keeping with its prevailing presentation to humans at the particular period. That is to say you have to attune yourself to however God appears as an Event coinciding with your Time and Place.*—Western Inner Workings, page 164

To better understand the mechanism of space, time, and event we need to understand the roles played by the soul and the host personality it inhabits. Earlier in the book I discussed the difference between the waking state and the dream state. This is very much like the relationship between the soul and the persona/personality. The latter experiences and reacts based upon human nature whereas the soul sorts through it all in search of the lesson to be gained and integrated. There are two different things happening as a result of the same event. The soul must correctly interpret the event. The success or lack thereof results in an energy emanation that flavors the spirit. It also colors the aura; it dissolves into the quintessence. When people read or sense someone's aura, they are feeling the results of the interplay between soul and spirit. The persona can pretend how it feels but the aura cannot reflect anything other than its energetic/spiritual condition.

The role of the persona is to experience finite reality, and through those experiences to challenge the soul's discernment. The persona symbolically represents what the soul has yet to fully understand and integrate into its being. It is a constant reminder and a teacher (as only a pupil can be). The soul symbolizes to the persona all that is worthy of attainment. For better or worse we all must deal with the struggle between soul and persona, spirit and body. It is all about movement and evolution through outgoing spirals of awareness and realization. The teaching we encountered earlier is that the Universe has no plans for our destruction; it has only plans for our successful spiritual evolution. This is key and central to the theme of reincarnation, the return of the soul to the experience of the body.

Everything that affects the soul affects the spirit, and what affects the spirit affects the body. In part, this causes a ripple that stimulates the Ancestral awareness of you. It is like a signal sent out from the DNA. The Dead are attracted as well. Have you ever noticed the phenomena that humans can be at their best when things are at their worst? At such times we can be heroic, actively compassionate, demonstratively generous, and completely selfless. Why do you suppose that is? Might it be our Ancestors and beloved Dead empowering us as allies from a higher plane of existence? Perhaps it may even be the soul taking the reins when the consciousness of the persona is stunned into inaction.

At the core of everything discussed in this chapter is the immeasurable value of communication. When our Ancestors created gestures and language, they were able to share information. They were able to inform others of things not directly experienced by those on the receiving end (there is food over there, a passage around this, enemies coming from that direction, etc.). The spiritual counterpart of this became mysticism, shamanism, mediumship, and even religion. Later in this book you will find several techniques that can help you communicate with those who have gone before you. Your Ancestors are further up the road you have yet to travel. You need their help to understand the journey you are on. Did you know that some of them need your help as well?

Healing the Ancestors

Many people carry regrets with them through life. This can be founded in the way they mistreated someone, things they never accomplished, or failures that defeated them. Regrets can also come from things we never took time for or from opportunities we let slip through our hands.

When I was a teenager I used to walk along the shore of Lake Ontario on a summer's morning. Each day I passed an old man sitting on a log as he looked out upon the water. We routinely exchanged a smile and a wave of the hand, and then one day I stopped to talk with him. I asked him what advice he might have for me as a young person. The old man replied: "There are many things I did and didn't do in my life. Now I've fewer years ahead of me than behind me. Every day I sit here thinking of what I never did in life. Advice? Live your life so that in the end it doesn't all come down to sitting on a log wishing you had lived your life more fully."

It is a metaphysical teaching that our life's "energy resonance" stays with us after the death process is completed. It adheres to the Spirit Body and is the "vibration" of the persona. This vibration is taken into the Ancestral Spirit because of its Earth Plane resonance. In other words it is attached to the same source of life that was part of our Ancestors' experience when they were living in human form. In metaphysics this is akin to the principle that "like attracts like." Therefore, the resonance of the persona, along with the sentience of the persona, is absorbed into the Ancestral Spirit. In effect a "copy" is left with the soul, which then assimilates this into its being. This is not unlike you having the experience and the memory of once being any given age in your life up until now.

As personas enter the Ancestral Realm, their energy imprint merges with the Ancestors. This in turn has an effect upon the consciousness and condition of the Ancestral Spirit. What is not commonly considered is that the vibration within the Ancestral Spirit also affects the living descendants. It is the metamorphic field and resonance mechanism operating within the Living River of Blood. This is not unlike the biblical principle that the "sins of the father" are punished on future generations, as found in Exodus 34:7, Numbers 14:18, and Deuteronomy 5:9 (among others). The primary difference is that in metaphysics there is no punishment and there is no reward. There is only the seeking of balance and harmony. Establishing that is not always an enjoyable experience.

It is the persona that acquires the resonance of positive and negative in a lifetime, but this does not exclude an impact upon the soul. The persona's resonance within the Ancestral Spirit is tethered to the soul, which can result in the soul being drawn back into specific bloodlines. The purpose is to either resolve the negative or to advance the positive. This is also true of any spiritual lineage as opposed to genetic lineage. For example, a soul born to Catholic parents can move with the persona as it converts at some point to another religion or spiritual path. After the death of the persona, the soul may discover this spiritual marker has a stronger pull on the reincarnating soul than does the genetic ties. The point to remember is that soul has a mission, and this mission takes priority over the vessel or the means it uses to accomplish it.

When the Ancestral Spirit moves to call a soul back, it is because a need exists to resolve or restore something; it can also intend to complete something unfinished in the lineage. A completion results in balance and harmony, which is the state of consciousness desired by the Ancestral Spirit.

Earlier in this section of the chapter I mentioned regrets. When a persona holds regrets or is troubled by its previous deeds in life, this affects the hive-mind of the Ancestral Spirit. The work of the incarnate soul is, in part, to heal the persona and/or the Ancestors who are in need of it. In some spiritual systems this is known as "redeeming" the Ancestors. This involves an offering or the performance of a service intended to "pay off a debt" or make amends on their behalf. In a later chapter you will find detailed information about how this works.

An excellent example of redemption appears in the *Lord of The Rings* movie trilogy. The hero Aragorn seeks out the ghosts of men who died cursed and ashamed for breaking an oath they took in life. He needs them to join in a great battle. To that end he promises to hold their oath as fulfilled if they come to his aid. This act promises to release them from remaining a cursed ghost army forever. They agree and fight for Aragorn, who honors his word, and in the end the Dead are redeemed. They vanish in glory from the battlefield and join their Ancestors.

One side benefit of healing or redeeming the Ancestors is that it liberates the soul of the person performing the act. For example, when my father (who was physically and emotionally abusive) died, I said to the "Universe" that if anything is owed by his spirit on account of his mistreatment of me, I cancel the debt. In that moment I felt his spirit lighten, and I also felt something lift off of me and dissolve away. It was an act of liberation for me, and the beginning of healing for him. However, on a larger scale, the inherited stream of abuse within the family lineage that touched his life was diminished. Forgiving those who abused him, and those who abused the abusers before him, changes the past. That is to say it changes the momentum, alters the morphic resonance, and redeems all generations (past, present, and future).

Look at events in the world today. Old and ancient feuds fuel violence, ill intentions, and warfare. Generations have been at war for centuries, and each new one is taught intolerance and vengeance. In this there is no peace or harmony for the Dead or for the Ancestors, no redemption. In return, the living generation has no healthy roots to draw upon for healing, no resonance to bring about change. It can only ingest the toxins left behind in the Ancestral Spirit.

The work of key souls in the living generation must be applied to the past and the present. The past must be re-envisioned so that the present is changed in accord. The living must do what the Dead failed to do, and the arriving soul must work to redeem the Ancestral Spirit; it and the Spirit of the Ancestral Lands must be purified. The living generation mistakes the voice of the Spirit of the Land as crying out for vengeance. It is the Dead who cry out to be avenged; the Ancestors call out for life as they have a vested interest in the Living. Part of that vested interest is in not being forgotten; for when something is forgotten, a part of the future dies with it.

CHAPTER 5

DEATH AND REBIRTH

Death has always been part of the human experience, and yet we struggle with it like no other situation in life. Most humans today see it as an ending, a permanent loss always attached to sorrow and pain. A less subjective view is that death is the completion of one form of existence that allows transition into the next phase (for the Higher, Middle, and Lower Selves). We grieve for our loss when someone we love dies, but this is a grief due to lack of physical presence. The loved one continues on; she or he is never truly disconnected.

Our Ancestors saw death in a more natural way than we do today. They lived in a world that demonstrated to them each year what the cycle of life is all about: birth, life, death, and renewal. The seasons taught them; the life of plants and animals taught them. Our Ancestors knew that humans are part of the cycle and the natural order of things. Unfortunately when the One God came to displace the Many, the vital and connecting component of "renewal" fell from sight. The circle was broken, the Ancestral gates were jammed close, and only the matter of the Dead remained. When death is taught as the end, the lives of people can be easily controlled through its fear. This is especially true when you add in a dismal and horrifying eternal consequence for not doing as you are told.

The good news is that the Universe has no plans for your demise, and there is no place set aside to torment you in for eternity. The other side of that coin is that no place of eternal reward awaits you either. What does await you is what naturally happens to all humans and all souls that inhabit them. It happened long before any religion or spiritual tradition. It is happening still: birth, life, death, and renewal.

Death is not only an event; it is a process as well. I stress this because I feel we need to return to the Ancestral view of death as a natural thing. Once we see death in this way, we can then begin to sort out what is natural and what is concocted through human design. Because death is actually about the body, let us begin there.

From a metaphysical perspective, the body is formed through the creative elements of Earth, Air, Fire, and Water. These not only initiate materialization through their presence, they also initiate decay when they withdraw from the body. In mundane science the process of forming a human body is limited to looking at fertilization, DNA, chromosomes, and cellular activity. In this view, the body is an assembly of atoms and molecules, and these are kept cohesive through the actions of electrons. However, electrons are also responsible for the degradation of the body when they initiate free radicals that damage cells.

One metaphysical thought is that bodies die in order to release souls back into the cycle of evolution. The physical science view is that bodies die because they deteriorate over time and can no longer sustain biological life. Another factor is, of course, death of the body due to injury. Injury to the soul can also result in the death of the body. This is reflected in the idea of people losing the will to live. The soul, while superior in consciousness to its human host, is not impervious to damage. Fortunately whatever happens to it is resolved over time.

Among the many teachings there is one stating that the process of death begins in the energy bodies before it does in the physical body. Some psychics believe they can "see" it in the aura. This is not unlike a doctor looking at a medical scan or X-ray and seeing a shadow that indicates a tumor. The underlying metaphysical principle is that things form in the non-material plane before they manifest in the Material Plane. Earlier in this book we saw a reflection of this principle in how a body is first envisioned in the Astral Plane, and then later condenses into a Material Body, a replica of the Energy Body.

Once death is unavoidable in the body, the energy bodies begin to wane. I often feel illness in someone's energy fields as a cold spot or a "pulling-in" area. This process is making way for the soul to be released from being bound to the flesh. The physical body draws upon the energy bands (described in Chapter Two) for sustainment as the organs begin to fail. This allows time for the soul to prepare to be "birthed" from the body. This is not unlike the fetus beginning to respond to the contractions of the womb as its birthing begins.

In physical death, rigor mortis is the mechanism, or contractions if you will, that serves to move the spirit and soul out of material captivity. Because there is no longer any energy being generated by the body, there is no likeness of energy to provide an environment conducive for the soul and spirit. This is like pouring out all the water from a fishbowl; the fish has lost what sustained it in the bowl. Rigor mortis begins 1–7 hours after death and disappears after 1–6 days, or when decomposition begins.

In one metaphysical belief the spirit is bound to the area where the body is located for up to seven days. The soul is still with the spirit during this time. Together they will learn important things about themselves by hearing what the Living have to say about them. It is something we all must face as we see ourselves as others did. The value of this is for the soul and the persona, for with it lays the ability to make changes. The persona remains as the being it was in life; that is to say it does not evolve on its own as can the soul. This is another reason why the work of the soul to redeem the Ancestors is important; the persona will one day become an Ancestor. There its consciousness can be enriched and elevated by Ancestors within the Collective who have already been liberated.

The late Dion Fortune, a renowned writer on metaphysical principles, provided some interesting insights into the process of dying and what follows after death. Of particular value is the section on the experience of those who are prepared to meet death and those who are not. She likens this to two men who take a sea journey. One is wealthy and educated about the destination; the other is a poor immigrant knowing little to nothing of the land to which he travels. The wealthy man enters the ship with joyful expectation while the immigrant enters with fear of what lies ahead.

Dion Fortune (as a Christian Mystic) points to a specific "angel" that she feels is attached to the death experience. Its alleged role is to place a deep sleep upon the fearful person as he or she passes from life. Fortune calls this entity The Great Anesthetist as well as The Angel of Death. In her view, the person later awakens in the death state and gradually becomes aware. When I first read this portion of her book, it reminded me of when I was young child. Sometimes I would wake up in my room and not know where I was; the room was unfamiliar. I think I may have even been uncertain for a moment as to who I was (but I was too drowsy to be alarmed). As I became more awake, everything slowly settled down and I understood my experience. Perhaps death is like that for some people.

At some point following the death of the body comes what is sometimes called "the second death." This is when the Higher Consciousness of the soul separates from the spirit (which carries the persona). The soul reclaims its inherent Higher Consciousness unhindered by its previous attachment, and the spirit remains in its "Lower" Consciousness. This results in a severance; it has died to the soul just as the body died to the spirit within it.

It is well-documented that a dying person often describes seeing departed loved ones in the room. Science ascribes this experience to changes in brain chemistry; metaphysics points to an opening between the material and non-material realms (through which the Dead arrive and we pass). I see no reason that one notion need negate the other. Perhaps the chemicals enhance our senses, and in this altered state of consciousness we possess the ability to see another spectrum. This is not entirely unlike the fact that we cannot see various spectrums of light that exist without the use of a device.

Do the Dead actually come to us in the hour of our death? Do our Ancestors gather as well? Whatever the case may be it seems reasonable (from a spiritual point of view) to think that something is there to usher us over to the "other side." Later we will explore that "place," but for now let us look closer at the concept of guides or companions.

Religions and spiritual systems have long taught of benevolent beings that comfort and aid humankind. They are called angels, spirit guides, guardians, and ascended masters. Such beings are believed to "look after" us during life and then see us through to the Afterlife. Beliefs in their actual role at the time of death vary from system to system. Some mystics believe that they take on the appearance of loved ones in order to make us feel safe as we cross from life. This is the idea that the familiar makes us feel comfortable and eases our anxiety.

For people who did not form loving relationships in life there may not be anyone whose greeting presence offers comfort on the other side. Another factor plays a role in this situation. Many people who were pronounced dead but came back to life report the presence of a bright warm light. This light feels loving, and often within it can be seen vague humanoid figures that seem present to welcome the Dead. The prevailing idea is that we are not alone in death just as we were not alone in birth; caretakers are there.

Dion Fortune writes:

> It is a great thing to know that as the physical world recedes from us, the coast of the next world is rising above the horizon of consciousness, and on that shore will be awaiting our coming all those who loved us and who have gone before us into the Unseen. We shall land amid familiar faces . . . but what of those who have no close ties with any in the next world . . . they will be met by those who knew unrequited love while on the earth.

The views of Dion Fortune, and many of the writers of her time, are vey simplistic and even poetic when it comes to the theme of dying and the Dead. Most of these commentators, being mystics, tended to bypass the importance of the Material Plane. Instead they favored the Spiritual Plane. Few distinguished the person from the soul, often regarding the reincarnated as being exactly the same person she or he was in the past life. It may boil down to semantics, but it does tend to somewhat muddy the waters as we try to sort things out.

In ancient myth and lore we often find the theme of the death crossing to a mystical island. It is typically a solo journey, and the Dead are met by mythical characters. Very often they are women commonly dressed in white or black. When arriving by boat, the vessel resembles a swan or some other being. The boat conveys the Dead to an island with white shores. A castle is present and usually appears in the center of the island. There are other themes in various cultures; some of them are not so pleasant.

The Landscape of the Afterlife

An important message in these old tales is the idea that the Dead leave; they go to another place. Attached to this theme is the fact that we must let them go in peace. While grief is natural for the Living, it can hold back the spirit (or even the soul) of the person from dissolving ties to the Earth Plane. The Material Plane is designed for material beings. The Spirit World is the Natural Plane for non-material beings. Over the centuries humans have imagined many realms residing in the Spirit World.

Many older cultures, particularly pre-Christian or non-Christian ones, thought of the Afterlife being much like the world of the Living (at least in the formative periods). Some examples are the "Happy Hunting Grounds" attributed to some American Indian tribes, the Elysian Fields of the Greeks, Mag Mell and Tír na nÓg of Celtic religion, and so on. The general theme is one of eternal summer and all its pleasure and bounty. Nordic and Germanic views are less clear in old literature, but in general the Afterlife is intimately connected to the material world and is "beneath it" (in other words, an Underworld Realm). In old tales we find references to the "hall of the fallen," the "field of the people," and the "field of the warriors." All of these have Earth Plane connections.

In old Chinese views of the Afterlife one's spirit is taken by messengers to the god of walls and moats, Ch'eng Huang, who reviews her or his life. If found virtuous, the soul can go directly to one of the Buddhist paradises, to the dwelling place of the Taoist immortals, or if not, it goes to the 10th court of hell for immediate rebirth. The latter is a temporary place of punishment. At the end of the term the soul drinks the elixir of oblivion and is placed on the Wheel of Rebirth.

Old Japanese views (primarily in Shinto religion) hold that after death the soul or spirit inhabits the Otherworld, where deities reside. There are several realms there, including Takamanohara (heaven, where the principal deities reside), Yomi (the Underworld and domain of the Divine mother of Japan), and the realm of Tokoyo (located somewhere beyond the sea). These worlds are much like earth in appearance; from a religious point of view they are neither a realm of rewarding paradise nor a punishing hell. The Afterlife is envisioned much like the world of the Living.

Over the course of time mystics inserted certain views and philosophies that shaped new thinking about the Afterlife. Mysterious islands, banquet halls, summer lands, and Underworlds gave way to the concept of inner planes of existence. One early model is the existence of four realms: Material, Lunar, Solar, and Stellar. Each represents a stage or phase of consciousness through which the soul evolves. Let us look at these worlds and their function in mystical thought.

The Material Realm, as we have seen, is where the consciousness is immersed in finite reality. It is the world of unyielding physical laws and principles. Like a person learning to crawl before walking, the soul is saddled with having to operate in a systematic existence. The flesh body must be mastered and then used to experience material reality. It is, in essence, the "deep-sea diving suit" of the soul; with it the soul explores the Earth Plane environment. The sea is an alien environment to air-breathing humans, and successfully exploring it requires the development of specific skills. It is the same for a soul in a flesh body in a material world. Such a realm offers lessons in fundamental and foundational understanding. All the myriad things taught in earthly existence can then be applied in expansive ways to other forms of reality.

The Lunar Realm is the Otherworld imagined through myth and legend. Its vibration or frequency is just above that of material form. The moon as seemingly being "above" the earth, and its characteristic changing of "body forms" (phase of the moon) may have contributed to assigning it to the next abode of the soul after death. In mystical thought, the Lunar Realm (not to be confused with the moon itself) is where souls reside that no longer require reincarnation (see subsection on reincarnation for clarification). It is here that the soul learns new lessons, and it learns how to apply material principles to non-material modes. One example is uncovering the forces within and behind material manifestations. This is similar to scientists discovering that material objects are not actually completely solid. Instead they are comprised of atoms and molecules, which have spaces between them. Material objects are masses of components that don't actually touch each other (and therefore are not solid in the way most people think). This opened up for scientists a more expanded view of material reality, which in turn led them to explore things like quantum fields and mechanics. This field offers us the view that nothing is actually as it seems.

The soul in the Lunar Realm learns about the forces that are behind formation and manifestation. It sees the layers, each one going deeper away from solidity and closer to pure energy. In this the soul encounters a different systematic reality than what it knew in the material world. It is no longer in an ocean; it is in a sea of atoms that respond to conscious direction and design. It is here that the process whereby "thoughts become things" functions as a mechanism. We no longer need to build with exterior materials; we create through holding in our consciousness the image of what we seek to manifest. The ability to wield this responsibly requires education and training, and so the Lunar Realm becomes a place of higher education once the soul has "graduated" from the school of the Material Realm.

Next in order of higher frequency/vibration is the Solar Realm. It is often regarded as the Plane of Forging. Its environment burns away material illusion and transforms lunar envisioning into Divine-like methodology. In other words it forges the soul's consciousness into a new "body" that operates within the Divine Plan. It is a consciousness that does not use or apply what was learned in Material or Lunar "classrooms" but instead merges with the universal consciousness of the "Great Instructor" itself. It is the difference between being a place of learning and being what is taught there.

In this newly forged consciousness of the Solar Realm, the soul reflects on what has been and what follows in accord with Divine Will. The self no longer exists in the Solar Realm as it did in the "lower" realms. It now knows itself as part of something greater than itself, that it is in service to as a being. With this realization, the vibration of the soul is heightened, and it is drawn upward to another plane of existence.

The last of the four realms is called the Stellar Realm. It is where we come full circle from point of origin to completion of cycle. There is a teaching that souls are sparks of consciousness sent out from the Source of All Things. In this light, you and I are the offspring of that which created the Universe. Some people say that the reason we stare at the stars is because we long for our true home.

In function, we can think of the Stellar Realm as the place where the collective experience of all souls is gathered and integrated. It is where we interface with the Source of All Things, and through the collective it knows all things. As mentioned earlier in the book souls travel in groups. These groups in turn belong to a greater Community, the Community of Souls. This is not unlike being residents of a state, which in turn is part of a country. I recall returning once from an unpleasant trip to another country. Even though my plane landed in California, I was happy to be back in America.

The longing of the soul to return to its natural realm is a driving force that inspires it to obtain liberation from the Cycle of Rebirth. Until then the soul will make many journeys using many vessels. Some journeys will be more memorable and transformative than others. Lifetimes may be long and others very short. In some cases incarnations take place to provide something for those individuals connected to the incarnate soul in its lifetime. Here the life is typically brief as in the death of an infant or a child.

In the Stellar Realm the next lifetime is projected. The soul obtains an overview, and through this it gains knowledge of what the life has to offer in terms of aiding spiritual evolution. It does not know everything the next incarnation offers, but in general the key elements become known. However, this is not destiny; it is instead opportunities.

While the incarnated soul will naturally move towards the glimpsed opportunities, there are factors that may impact accomplishing the goals. We can take comfort in the fact that the Source of All Things is exceedingly patient, and we have all the time needed to complete our successful spiritual evolution.

Reincarnation: The Call to Return

In a previous chapter we explored the general role of reincarnation. In this section we will look at some particular elements. What initiates the process of reincarnation, and do we have any choices in the matter? Are we subject to reincarnation or do we willing participate? These questions open us up to a fascinating journey.

It is clear that reincarnation joins a soul with a Material Body. Since the soul preexists the body, let us begin our exploration with the material form into which the soul will pass. The body is composed of various elements that come together to create it. This creation, from cell to organism, relies upon a harmonious and unified process. If everything works together, then the body is created as per the intended design. If not, the creation may not happen or it may be flawed in one way or another.

There is an ancient Greek myth about Creation that captures this overall theme. The myth tells us that before Creation all was in chaos. Chaos reigned because the four creative elements of Air, Fire, Water, and Earth were not operating in unison and harmony. Each was solely focused and not in relationship with the process of Creation. The myth tells us that the fifth element of Spirit (aether) entered into the chaos and drew the Four Elements together in harmony and commonality of purpose.

If we apply the model of the Four Elements and Spirit to the process of reincarnation and the body, then something interesting comes into view. A metaphysical teaching is that our bodies come together due to elemental forces. In other words the Four Elements join in unison to initiate and complete the process whereby our material bodies are fashioned. The activity of the Elements stimulates the awareness of the soul in the higher planes, just as in the Greek myth in which the fifth element is aware of the Elemental activity. This activity, the formation of the body, signals a response from the soul. An opportunity for the soul is forming; through it growth and evolution are available. Also offered is the role of redeemer of the Ancestors through the bloodline lineage of the body the soul will inhabit. But how much if any does the soul have to say in the matter?

It is commonly said in mainstream culture that birth is not the choice of the newborn; it was the choice of the parents. We looked at the Elemental role, which suggests that the formation of the body draws the soul. However, might it be that the soul first initiates the formation of the body when it has need or desire for reincarnation? Are we arguing which came first, the chicken or the egg?

One metaphysical view is that once the soul has completed an incarnation and delivered its experience to the Source of All Things, it rests. This rest is not one born of fatigue; the rest is one of contemplation and reflection. It reviews the past life, integrates it into the whole of all its experiences with other incarnations, and then opens itself to Divine Consciousness. Through directly communing with Divine Consciousness the soul is enlightened as to the next phase of its evolution. This is not so unlike a college counselor helping you to understand what courses you still need to take for your major in the upcoming semesters.

A little known teaching is that reincarnation begins with communion between a soul and the Ancestral Spirit. The bond is there because the soul was embodied in many of those who are now the Ancestors with the Ancestral Realm. Here the "discussions" take place about possible next lifetime opportunities and what they offer. It is not unlike a well-known actor being offered movie roles and reading the movie scripts. Sometimes the soul is the star, and other times it is a supporting actor; or it might even be a character who ends up not being all that memorable in the movie.

A teaching here is that the soul can gain an overview of the next lifetime. It sees the possibilities, the benefits, and the potential. The risks and challenges also become known to the soul. Little, if anything, is certain to occur in this vision once the soul is embedded in a flesh body. There are primary markers such as social status, marriage, children, health or lack thereof, and death. This last approaches at certain intersections in a lifetime when it is likely to occur; but the exact date is not sitting on a calendar ahead of time. One valuable guide map for the soul is the Natal Chart in Astrology. It is, in essence, a reference guide to the previously mentioned markers. With this foreknowledge we can move forward into territory that might otherwise be completely unknown.

Once the soul has accepted a new role, the Ancestors stimulate the forces that will eventually manifest a new body—the Elemental Body. They can do so because they are essentially in-between the Earth Plane and the Elemental Plane; therefore they are connected to both spheres of influence. The Ancestral influence, through energetic action, establishes the resonance that will cause the Elemental Body to form around a genetic lineage whose energy pattern (or imprint) is held in the Ancestral Spirit. In this way the Elemental Body will carry the DNA resonance, giving a nationality to the body. This is part of the metaphysical principle that states "like attracts like." The partnership between the soul and the Ancestors is bound to this process, and from the ancient pool of light a flame of Human Consciousness is sent to join the body. All that remains is for the soul to take up residence and begin a new lifetime journey.

From a mystical perspective the soul moves from the Stellar Realm and begins its journey into the Material Realm. The Lunar Realm reacts to the "astral" (meaning star-like) resonance of the soul and lends its substance to coat it with a spirit form body. Remember that earlier we connected the Ancestors (and the Dead) to the Lunar Realm. Therefore the Ancestors are aiding in directing this process of forming the Energy Body through Elemental forces. This will become the Material Body once the energy is condensed by the resonance of the Material Realm. You can envision this like putting your hand in a bowl of melted wax; the wax will form around the hand (essentially making a replica of what was introduced into its substance—your hand).

Once the soul enters into a flesh body in its fetus stage, the Higher and Lower Selves join together in a relationship of interconnected consciousness. This is formed first before Human Consciousness appears as the persona. Until that time the Elemental Body is growing in the womb with its own consciousness, which is evidenced in the generation of cells and the formation of organs, and so on. The persona (the human mind) is not controlling or directing this process of creating a fetus. It has yet to come forth and form a triad with the body and soul. An idea we will later explore is that communication between the soul and the body is always directly through the body as opposed to through Human Consciousness. This reflects the initial first bonding of consciousness between the body and soul. It does not need to remain this way, but more about that later on.

One intriguing teaching is that the "way of return" is connected to what is called the Star Gates, or the Four Gates of Atavaric Descent. The related teaching is that some souls have evolved beyond the need to return to the material, but they choose to come back in order to help those souls who struggle with liberation. These advanced souls, known as avatars, are said to enter the mortal world through the fixed signs of the zodiac: Aquarius, Taurus, Leo, and Scorpio. These are symbolized by the images of man, bull, lion, and eagle. This set of four beings appears in various mystical and occult teachings.

Not all souls that pass into the Material Realm through the Four Gates are advanced souls. Avatars use the fixed star signs (representing the gates) because the quality of a fixed sign bestows strength of purpose, which propels them to complete their mission. A companion teaching is that the descending soul passes through the Solar Realm, which imprints it with a "sun sign" as shown in the Natal Chart of Astrology. This becomes the energetic resonance of the soul on the Earth during a lifetime. It is also a spiritual map in the mystical sense.

The sign of Aquarius, representing Human Consciousness, gives the avatar the energy of the pioneer or trailblazer. Taurus establishes the form through which the avatar will present its teachings. Leo instills the creativity that inspires expansion, the opening of minds and hearts. Scorpio offers the commitment to the spiritual path that the avatar will walk. It may well be that the avatar is a soul that passes through each of the Four Gates before its final role as a spiritual master.

In a mystical view the four creatures of man, bull, lion, and eagle represent the traits that are necessary to build new worlds and to bring about positive and beneficial change. It is all about communication and the interplay of forms of consciousness that meet and act in mutual agreement. From this arises the power and resonance of three consciousnesses acting as one: body, mind, and soul.

The Triad of Consciousness: Body, Mind, and Soul

In this section we will explore the different "conscious beings" within us and through which you and I experience and work with in each lifetime. The overall purpose is to aid growth and evolution. Existence is not still and inactive. As beings in the midst of it all, of we too share that same nature, quality, or condition. In this light, Elemental Consciousness is elevated as is Human and Soul Consciousness.

You may never have thought of the body as a separate being from the "you" that you believe yourself to be in the here and now. In this light, mystics promote the idea that when you are injured, do not say "I am in pain" but instead say "my body" is experiencing pain. This mindset keeps the two distinct. This is easier to understand if you take note that a painkiller only makes the mind become unaware or less aware of the pain; the body is still in the same pain situation of the material reality that is generating the pain. In this same light, do not say that you are ill or do not feel well. Instead, say that your stomach is upset or that your body has flu symptoms. This may come across as a game, but it is not. Its value is in keeping each of the three consciousnesses operating true to their intended roles.

The body is the way that Elemental Consciousness experiences a sensory reality. This elevates it through having to deal with the unique mechanisms of a flesh form as opposed to a simply energetic one (its former state). This is, in effect, the difference between theory and practice. You can read everything written about sailing a boat, but until you sail there is no realization (there is only knowledge). Knowledge gives you options but realization calls for focused action. Knowledge is like sitting on a train track knowing that a train is due to arrive soon. You have options: sit longer or get up. Once the train is bearing down on you, realization makes you act immediately. In this light we can say that the Elemental Body is here to realize the other half of existence, which is material reality.

On another level the role of the Elemental Body is to convert food into energy; this energy is used by Human Consciousness that inhabits it. The Elemental Body can do this because it originated as energy that was transmuted into material; it remembers its primal state and has not lost connection to it or its processes. At death the elements withdraw back into their original state, and this is when decomposition begins.

Human Consciousness inhabits the Elemental Body. It is seeded from the Ancestral Spirit, planted within the joining of the soul and the Elemental Body. This is much like the joining of a sperm with an egg that brings about the formation of a fetus. Through Ancestral connection to many incarnations Human Consciousness can attain a higher vibration and become a strong presence in the Ancestral Realm. From time to time these elevated Ancestral beings attach themselves to a human life and have significant impact on human culture, religion, and spirituality. Not all humans are reincarnations of past ones on this Earth; some human bodies carry souls from other dimensions such as the Faery Realm, or from other planets; but this does not concern us here in this chapter. It does, however, help us not to be confused by the fact that our planet has over 7 billion human bodies living on it, which is more humans than all previous time periods combined up until this current one.

Soul Consciousness completely envelops the Elemental Body (and its energy fields) but is centered or anchored in the area of the solar plexus. That is to say it is here the soul affixes to, and interfaces with, the flesh body and Human Consciousness. The soul takes in energy through the solar plexus from within the bound atmosphere of the Earth. It uses this in the same way the flesh body uses food and water.

The three different "beings of consciousness" come together to accomplish a mutual transformation that benefits each one. Each one originates from a stream of life-forms moving along with the current of evolution. Together they bind into one triformis nature, a single being comprised of three separate ones. The body is the vessel, the soul is the navigator, and the Human Consciousness is the pilot. In unison they reach their destination through cooperation. However, pilot error can change everything. Proper communication is vital.

Communication among the Selves

As previously noted, communication occurs naturally between the Lower Self and the Higher Self. We have referred to this as the Elemental Body and the soul. Human Consciousness must work with effort to directly communicate with the Higher Self. This is because of the three types of consciousness only the Middle Self can vary from its design and become conflicted. The Lower Self takes everything literally and responds in conformity with what it receives. The results are health or illness. The Higher Self is incapable of victimization and cannot be self-deceptive. Only the Middle Self can misinterpret its reality.

In order to better understand the relationship of the Three Selves, we can look at the imagery of the lover's card in the tarot. Because the old symbolism has morphed over time, I will use the Waite-Rider card that retains the esoteric imagery. Love, being an intimate relationship, is an ideal theme for looking into communication of body, mind, and soul. Let's examine the symbolism on this card in context with the teachings of the Three Selves.

The sun sitting overhead represents the radiant energy from which all beings derive their own inner force. It also represents the "guiding light" of ageless wisdom and is a sign to all below it of the unlimited potential of consciousness for all beings. The winged being in the upper center represents the higher consciousness. It is also the power of air as thought and the communication forces under the planet Mercury. Mercury is associated with the astrological sign of Gemini, which for our purposes here signifies twins—the material and spiritual (as above, so below).

The cloud formation directly in the center position represents the "Life-Breath" that is also known as Prana in Eastern Mysticism. Earlier in this chapter we noted that the Higher

Self is connected to the body at the solar plexus and is nourished by the intake of this Prana substance. The winged being (settled into the clouds) holds it hands outward to downpour its influence upon the two humanoid figures below it.

On the left is depicted a woman, who in our scenario represents the Elemental Body. She looks up at the winged being, which represents the soul, and this posture shows her in direct communication with it. The figure on the right is depicted as a man, and he represents the Middle Self, the Human Consciousness. The Middle Self communicates with the Higher Self through the Elemental Body. The man looks at the female figure indicating direct communication with the Material Body. The soul, raising a hand over each of the figures, shows its unconditional love for both of the other components of the triformis consciousness. The mountain in the background represents the journey that awaits the three conscious Selves, and the upward climb of evolution.

Pictured with the woman on the card we see a tree with a serpent on it. Paul Foster Case, an acknowledged authority on tarot symbolism, refers to the snake as the Serpent of Redemption. Case links it to the theme of Moses lifting up a serpent on a pole to redeem the Israelites of their sins (as told in the Old Testament, Numbers 21:4–9). In the New Testament, John 3:14, a connection is made between the lifting up of the serpent and the lifting up of Jesus on a wooden cross (made from a tree) to redeem the sins of all. From an esoteric perspective we can see the basic theme of redeeming the Ancestors, which we explored earlier in the book. In chapter one, we encountered the tree in connection with death and the rebirth in the Material Realm. We also looked at human lineage recorded in a family tree design. You may want to review that chapter again.

The man on the tarot card is shown with another tree. It bears twelve fruits of fire, which represent the stars of the zodiac. Case refers to it as the tree of human life upon which the personalities (persona) or "self-conscious life-expressions" blossom. The man on the card is called "the namer of things" and in this we see that Human Consciousness is fully immersed in material existence to the point of distraction. Therefore there is little wonder that the Middle Self communicates through the body to the Higher Self.

The esoteric message is about the "union of opposite but complementary modes of existence," as Case puts it. The underlying intelligence works to maintain a distinction between the Three Selves in terms of discernment. It is through discernment that the selves are arranged; to each one is apportioned its measure. Balance is the key, for if balance is disturbed then dis-ease occurs. This condition in turn begins to weaken or even dissolve the bonds that keep the Three Selves functioning in harmony as one.

The goal of communication is to master the body through some type of discipline, which will make Human Consciousness join with its organic host in a way that makes it then work as one being. One example is the martial arts. For many years I practiced Chinese Kenpo. Eventually the movements of my body blended with my consciousness to the degree where both reacted simultaneously to an event. There were still two distinct components at work, my mind and body, but each one fully trusted the other in communication. In time a spiritual condition arose which influenced my practice and discipline. It changed my body into an energy as opposed to my awareness of it as an object, and transformed my Human Consciousness from a "warrior" into a full participant in my life and its application. A warrior fights for a cause; a soul transcends the cause for a fight.

I learned to fight effectively, and in doing so the need and the desire to fight disappeared. There is a formula behind this outcome. The Higher Self influenced both the body and Human Consciousness, and this was made possible by the latter communicating to the Higher Self through the body. The body said, "I am whole, loyal, dependable, and true," and through the body the Middle Self said, "with my body I am without fear, and I am fearless to live." The soul replied: "Let us move forward with unconditional love." In this the three conscious Selves offered no conflict to each other. Communication was within a cycle, a wheel within a wheel. Any of these inner voices could speak in any order, and the message went unchanged at its core. Try rearranging these three statements together in a different order, and see how the message does not change but expands. When the message goes unchanged in the threefold consciousness, we have arrived at the threshold of enlightenment.

You can use other disciplines to create effective ways for Human Consciousness to communicate with the body. You might try yoga, meditation, dance, or other things that require a strong connection between mind and body. Solitary endeavors seem to work best as opposed to team sports. The less outside distraction, competition, or stimulation, the better the results will be. Remember, you are not the body; it is its own being. You are the director guiding it into a mutually beneficial relationship that is a full-time commitment.

In order to better understand the three-way communication, let us look at the inner mechanism. Human Consciousness forms and maintains the persona of the individual. As we noted earlier, it is in constant communication with the body, but this does not mean that it is not receiving direct communication from the soul. The problem is in the personality transmitting and not receiving from the soul.

The soul communicates directly with Human Consciousness in the dream state. This is often thought of as the subconscious mind operating when we are asleep. It takes discernment to differentiate between a dream that arises from the consciousness of the Elemental Body and that of a communication in the dream state directly from the soul. In most cases the dream is fragmented, while in the case of the soul, the dream seems very real. This is because the soul is bringing the consciousness of the persona into a relatively lucid state.

Developing the skill of lucid dreaming can help the persona to transmit directly to the soul without requiring the Elemental Body as the conduit. This is not an easy skill to develop, and in terms of meaningful and effective communication with the soul it can be problematic. The important thing is to listen as well as speak. The soul is an aid to evolution and not a fulfiller of wishes. The relationship between the soul and the persona needs to be an open and honest one with the goal being spiritual evolution.

The easiest way for Human Consciousness to work out any problems regarding soul communication is to call upon the Ancestors. As previously noted the soul and the Ancestors were in communication in the early stages of reincarnation. You have a direct link to them through your DNA (review Chapter Two). The ladder-like appearance of the DNA double helix is a symbol through which you can descend into the Cavern of the Ancestors. This is a spiritual corridor, a meeting point, through which the Ancestors can be directly approached. You can find a technique for this in Chapter Seven.

Rebirth: The Incarnate State

The end result of the process of reincarnation is, of course, the Material Body. As noted earlier it develops when the Ancestral Spirit joins with the soul in a quest of evolution and redemption. There is an element here of the principle called "karma," which is a tenet that comes from Eastern Mysticism. Like many foreign imports it is not a perfect fit for Western metaphysical teachings that originate from the European Ancestors.

In this book we have spent a significant amount of time forming the idea of Elemental, Human, and Soul Consciousness. Now it is time to focus on the experience of the persona in the material world. Human Consciousness as the personality in any given lifetime inevitably wonders about the meaning and purpose of life. Here it encounters the Three Great Mysteries— where did I come from, why am I here, and what happens when I die? I think that humans may spend more time wondering if life serves a reason and purpose than they do savoring the "gift of pure being" bestowed upon them.

From a metaphysical perspective you and I exist as humans for three basic purposes. We are here in the Ancestral stream to fulfill the will of our lineage. We are here to experience the Material Realm for the solid lessons it has to teach us so that we aid the evolution of our souls, and so we share consciousness with the Ancestral Spirit while we are in a flesh body. Lastly, we are here to communicate our perceptions of material existence back to the Creator/Creatrix so as to inform it with a constant stream of consciousness. Each of the Three Selves is attached to one of these roles. The Elemental Body is tied to the Ancestral stream, Human Consciousness to communication with the Source of All Things, and the soul to the evolution of consciousness and being. This is not only for itself (the soul) but for the gain this brings to the beings of the body and mind as well. While we assign these roles and purposes individually, all three consciousnesses are mutually sharing and benefiting from them in a simultaneous fashion.

In the course of life we are not limited to these three specific roles. There are many sub-roles operating as well. For example, our lives have an impact on the lives of people around us. So we can say that another role we play in life is to be one of the lessons that others encounter. The resonance of our personas draws us together through what is needed in that scenario. Our presence and activity can be purposeful or coincidental. This seems evident in the fact that we can make mistakes or cause someone pain through error as opposed to intentional design. I do not believe that everything is preordained, but I do believe there is an incredible mechanism at work that moves, sorts, and connects things together as life unfolds in front of us all. This is not performed in a "puppet master" way; it is done through action and reaction, cause and effect, but with the added element of conscious observation and awareness. This is not unlike a chess master in the midst of an ever-changing board where pieces are moving; some are under his direct control while other pieces are not. There is, however, still the attentive consciousness that makes it all one thing operating in a relationship of time, space, and event.

An important mechanism for Human Consciousness is the ability to control or influence environment. This helps to minimize "random occurrence" in one's life. One basic example is that having a home to be in at night minimizes the things that can happen to you in the world that evening. That particular environment is largely under your control for the time being. If you had no place to stay and were living out on the streets, your experience of random occurrence would be greatly increased as many things might happen to you that are outside of your control. In fact, that particular environment is controlling your experience of it.

The environments that we find ourselves in can greatly affect us. This includes being in the company of friends, family, lovers, and even coworkers. Their words, feelings, moods, and behaviors can change our very own in the moment. This can be either positive or negative, but the point is that it changes the energy (whether we want it to or not). This is why our consciousness should be developed to the point that we can maintain our state of being despite the energy projected on us. It is a question of balance.

Because our environment can impact us without our consent, it is empowering to be able to influence it and thereby cease its ability to influence us. This requires tapping into our center, the place of balance. We often feel a disruption at this center in a tense, stressful, or uncomfortable situation. It manifests in the area of the stomach and solar plexus; some people describe it as a knot in the stomach. In essence that is what it is, an energy knot that is hindering the flow of your natural balanced energy.

When we maintain our balance and temper our reaction to changes in environment, we then make changes to the environment around us. It stabilizes the forming environment, and then our resonance can ripple outwards through it and thereby introduce a new one. Meeting anger with anger, hatred with hatred, and loathing with loathing does not change the environment; it only strengthens it and its influence on everyone in that energy field. These qualities are primal and reflect our fears. It is Human Consciousness that must take the reins and establish harmony within the Elemental Body. To do so strengthens the bonds between us and the Ancestors because it is about growth and evolution. Once these bonds are in harmony, the soul quells the inner conflicts and disturbance.

If we extend this principle further out from the immediate environment, we then come to the state of being of our own lives. What is the environment that we call our lives? Do we feel resentful, victimized, persecuted, or held back? Do we feel sorry for ourselves? If so we have lost sight of the fact that the lessons we need to learn are the reasons these very things impact our lives. The good news is that we are not meant to suffer, we are meant to be transformed by it all.

Instead of wailing against our lot, if we accept it as meaningful to change, then interesting things begin to develop. One of the hardest things to do is to accept that the negative condition of our lives is justified. In other words, what we did or failed to do brought about the condition of this lifetime. It need not all have been in this lifetime, but can be carried over from a previous existence. If we can stop feeling wronged long enough to accept that we are not victims but full participants, then the bonds of "karma" begin to weaken. When we accept responsibility, then we come into favor with what some people call the Lords of Karma. This in turn lessens the intensity and tenacity of delivering the needed lessons to us.

Positive energy displaces negative energy when we do not lay responsibility on another person even when that person truly wronged us. To see ourselves as blameless only serves to maintain the imbalance that holds us to the negativity. If instead we acknowledge our role, we can begin to dissolve the bonds. Perhaps our role in the matter was that we trusted someone who was unworthy of that trust. Maybe we allowed a wrong or injustice to occur because we didn't react properly in a situation, and we allowed someone to take advantage of us in our weakness or confusion. It may also be that we put ourselves in danger or vulnerability, which allowed someone to harm us. When we do not remove ourselves from the equation, we can then heal the inner environment of our lives. Such a healing ripples all the way back to our Ancestors.

As you may be beginning to see, this is all about intentional consciousness, directed thought, for thoughts are things. Being in the flesh allows consciousness to create on the Material Plane. One of the things we can apply is known as the Law of Compensation. The only constant thing in the Universe is change. Therefore to hold to the idea that we can never accomplish this or that, or that we will never have this or that, is contrary to the process of existence itself. Nothing stays the same, so why hold ourselves to self-deception? To do so does not help us evolve, and does not help us redeem.

The Law of Compensation works as follows. If someone steals your cell phone, instead of focusing on the loss, you call for compensation instead. You sit, focus your mind, and request "of the Universe" that you obtain a cell phone that is the model up. In this way you move the energy forward; you do not bring it back to where it was because that negates the law of change. Acknowledge your loss and then request compensation. You can, and should, do this with all aspects within your life experience. This not only serves you, it serves the Ancestors by improving the way for the next generation through you (if not physically then spiritually). Who knows how the changes you make in the environment will affect the forward-flowing stream itself? Dare to master your environment; dare to be fulfilled and abundant. You are the hope of the Ancestors; you are their champion in this lifetime.

CHAPTER 6

Ancestors and the Serpent Wisdom

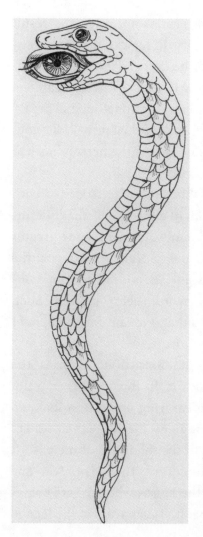

We are all aware of the statement "get off my back" and its meaning of being driven or hounded by others. We often regard the situation as one of being criticized, but there is another "back-rider" to examine; it is a spiritual concept. One teaching is that we are accompanied in life by one of the Ancestors from the collective of the Ancestral Spirit. This being is sometimes called the Mind-Rider or Spirit-Rider (I prefer the latter term). As mentioned in the Preface to this book, the Spirit-Rider shares a common quality with the Mayan Vision Serpent.

The Spirit-Rider is an Ancestor that can come and go between the Mortal Realm and the Ancestral Realm. It is said to attach itself to the spine of the descendant and to ride with her or him. The Spirit-Rider is seen as a serpent in replica form resembling the shape of the human spine; its head is positioned with the so-called primitive brain associated with the area of the brain stem. The Spirit-Rider does not always remain with the host body, but can and does rejoin the Ancestors in their realm from time to time.

One of things the Spirit-Rider does is called fetching; this means it can take our consciousness to another place or realm. Spiritual or magical visions are often the result of being fetched away. The Spirit-Rider can also fetch another Ancestor and bring it to the descendant. Without understanding "the fetch" and how it works, a person can feel psychotic or as if going through an emotional/mental breakdown. Fortunately most of the work of the Spirit-Rider goes unnoticed to the conscious mind unless the person has had some training or alignment practice.

There is one exception to this, and it is associated with what some people call the "chill of affirmation" that is a tingling feeling up the spine. It manifests when some greater truth is acknowledged in our being. This sensation is the Spirit-Rider moving in the spine; it is drawing our consciousness to appreciate the words being spoken. Such communication is from the soul and meant for the benefit of Human Consciousness.

From the mystical view the Spirit-Rider carries the "Ancestral Eye of the Past" with it. In this context, mystics envision the Rider as a snake carrying one eye in its open mouth. Through this, and through us, it can see the world of the Living, and it can help us to see the world of the past. It can also give us vision into the future. The idea of "the one eye" shows up in the myth of the Norns who are Fate beings in the lore of Northern Europe. It also appears in the legend of Perseus who encounters three sorceresses who share one eye that can be passed around between them. Perhaps the mythical theme of the "one eye" is a remnant of very old beliefs about Ancestral vision.

The Ancestral Eye of the Past allows us to look upon the world of Ancestral wisdom, to see it as it was in its day, and to see it as it is within us now. The eye travels on the breath of life to connect to an Ancestral descendant. Once attached, it looks out through the brow into the outer light. In some mystical systems this area is called the Third Eye and is located in the center of the forehead just above the eyebrows.

One of the teachings in the old Huna system is that a Kahuna has an etheric extension from the tailbone of the spine. It is thought of much like a lizard's tail, meaning that if severed it can rejuvenate. This tail keeps the Kahuna rooted in the Ancestral connection, rooted in communication with the past. In this we can see the etheric serpent that moves between the worlds.

Since encountering this teaching, I have come to feel that the sensation called "the chill of affirmation" is part of the shaman's tail mechanism. As previously mentioned, the "chill" is a tingling or wave-like sensation that runs up or down the spine when we are talking about something meaningful or spiritual. It often comes with a revelation about some matter in our life. From a metaphysical perspective it is an affirmation from "spirit" that truth has been spoken or experienced; it is the Higher Self sending the message to pay particular attention.

From time to time in life we can lose the feeling of spiritual connection, of connection to many things in our life. We can liken this to losing our tail, losing our rootedness to the Spirit of the Land, to the Ancestral Spirit. In time we can return to our Path or to what carries us forward in life. It is the tail regrown; it is the Ancestral vestige renewed.

It can be of comfort to know that we have a Spirit-Rider with us. It means we are not alone and not disconnected from those who came before us in our lineage. To have a Spirit-Rider means that an intentional process is at work within us, there is meaning and purpose to our lives. Like the serpent, however, it slips away from time to time; it disappears into an underworld. It seemingly leaves us for a time and then returns again. Like the sun, the moon, and the stars, its light goes into the West and disappears on the horizon. The Ancestral wisdom knows that light is at home in the darkness, and this is represented by the celestial lights passing above our world; they visit but do not stay, they return home when all is said and done.

Serpents Within and Without

In what can be called the Old Faiths of pre-Christian times we find the theme of Cosmic Serpent or World Serpent. This serpent is a mover of tides, and can be seen as those very tides. In this light the serpent originates and maintains the tides; more specifically it carries the tides of life and death. In the lore of this great serpent it is Divine in nature. This belief later morphed through Judaic-Christian influences that succeeded in minimizing its prior significance, and in vilifying its nature and character. However, remnants for the Old Faith can be found in the class of angels known as the Seraphim. The ancient Book of Enoch mentions them, and this is associated with the old depiction of the Seraphim as fiery serpent beings that serve as guardians.

In Ancestral wisdom the serpent is venerated, in part, because it moves easily between a variety of worlds and inner dimensions. It is the messenger between the material world and the non-material world; between the world of mortalkind and spirits of the Otherworld. In ancient artwork and myth the serpent is carried by a god or goddess. Two figures stand out in terms of being intimately connected with the Dead, and by extension to the Ancestors. They are the deities known as Hecate and Hermes. In addition to being associated with the Dead both of the deities bear serpents. The serpent is often depicted as a chthonic creature connected to the Underworld. In an earlier chapter we noted the serpent as the guardian of the seed, a metaphor for the assurance of continued generations.

In classic iconography Hecate holds a serpent in her hand, or is accompanied by one. Hermes appears with a caduceus that features two serpents climbing a staff. In metaphysical circles this is often linked to the double helix figure of DNA, which resembles two climbing serpents. Hermes is, among other things, a god who guides and escorts the Dead. As such he is known as the god of otherworldly boundaries and the transformation of souls. On an interesting side note, I previously mentioned the beehive as a symbol of the Ancestral Spirit; in one ancient myth Hermes is given a gift of bees by Apollo. Both bees and spirits of the Dead are associated with oracle abilities. Seeing into the future is a theme we saw regarding the soul and the Ancestral Spirit working together in the process of reincarnation as the joining of the terrestrial and celestial. Noteworthy is the fact that in the earliest depiction of Hermes he is dressed in a black garment decorated with stars (the original home of all souls).

Scholar Karl Kerenyi describes Hermes as calling the Dead (before burial) and putting them into a type of slumber with his golden staff. This is reminiscent of what Dion

Fortune called The Great Anesthetist (see Chapter Five). However, the Hermes that Kerenyi speaks of also awakens the Dead and opens a way to be released from the realm of the Dead. His winged caduceus uplifts the departed soul and guides it back amidst the stars. The twin serpents on his staff carry the Ancestors and call to the soul to return.

As noted in Chapter One, the serpent has long been associated with Ancestral veneration. Its winding movement represents the flow of the generations across time. The shedding of its skin symbolizes the many forms shed in the lifetimes that rise and recede in the course of time. In this light we can also view the serpent as a symbol of the Cosmic Life Force.

Anthropologist Jeremy Narby, in his book *The Cosmic Serpent: DNA and the Origins of Knowledge*, reveals a generational connection between DNA and communication between the body and the mind. Narby lived among a tribe of Peruvian Indians and was introduced to a plant substance called ayahuasca, which is effective and powerful at creating altered states of consciousness. Under the direction of shamans, Narby drinks the ayahuasca and experiences the inner realms and communication it offers. In particular he meets a large multicolored serpent that introduces itself as the creator of all things. Narby later concludes that ayahuasca can bring a person into direct communication with his or her DNA, which is represented by the serpent. An interesting connection arises when Narby learns that as DNA replicates, an intense photon particular bombardment occurs in the form of a multicolored snake-like ripple. Is this the serpent that Narby met, and who proclaimed itself the Creator?

Narby points out that many shamanic people use images other than a serpent when they work with non-material realms (or altered states of consciousness). Items or objects such as ropes, ladders, vines, or bridges/stairways are also used to enter other worlds. Some of these worlds are underneath the land while others are in the heavens above. Using these tools the shaman can enter a world usually traversed only by the Dead. The Gateway to this world is through the core concept known as the *axis mundi*, the axis of the world. Unlike the Dead, the shamans return to the world of the Living with conscious knowledge of the inner realms. This knowledge can be used for healing the mind and body.

Shamans of an Amazon tribe known as the Ashaninca teach about a "sky rope" that connects the earth and sky together. A copyrighted image of it appears in Narby's book (on page 94); the sky rope looks exactly like the double helix structure of DNA (the only difference being that it is somewhat stretched out). Narby's book also shows a photo of the plant from which the ayahuasca potion is made; the branches of this plant appear like two entwined serpents. The native users of the plant (*Banisteriopsis caapi*) call it the "spirit vine" and "the ladder to the Milky Way"—ayahuasca is called the "vine of the soul." Let's take a moment to look at the relevancy of all of this to the theme of Ancestors, communication, and spiritual evolution.

In previous chapters I wrote about the three types of consciousness we have while possessing a Material Body. For the purpose of this chapter we can look at the flesh body as being the serpent consciousness (by way of the DNA that formed it in the Material Plane). In this regard it is the rope or stairway connecting above and below, the body and the soul. This suits the concept we explored in other chapters that direct communication with the soul is through the body. Altered states of consciousness are reached through the body whether by ecstatic dance or ingesting or smoking a particular substance. The serpent-like DNA within our bodies connects us directly with the Ancestors.

Altered states of consciousness draw Human Consciousness into play, but are also a means for the soul to experience the flow between material and non-material existence all in one setting. It is like being able to observe the waking and the dream state all at once, or the interaction of the so-called conscious and subconscious states as one communication. In previous chapters we looked at the dream state as always in transition of forms and themes, while the waking state perceived reality as stable and linear (with the constancy of cause and effect unfolding before us in orderly ways). Imagine being the overseer and director of each one. Your soul is precisely that, but Human Consciousness is only self-aware and egocentric to and in the moment. This separates our levels of being, and there is a disconnect between the celestial and terrestrial partnership. One example is, oddly enough, found in the myth of Adam and Eve and the talking snake.

In the tale of the Garden of Eden we find Eve approaching the Tree of the Knowledge of Good and Evil. It is guarded by a serpent, as most trees with the power to transform usually do possess guardian snakes in old myths and legends. Eve, who we can assign to the Elemental Body, is instructed to not eat the fruit of this tree. In other words she is to remain without personal discernment; she is conscious only of being. This is the state of the Lower Self without the direction of Human Consciousness.

In our retelling of the story, "God" is the Higher Self trying to separate the Lower Self (the body) from communicating upward what it is not acclimated to comprehend, hence the order to not eat from the tree, or even touch it. This is attached to our earlier theme that the Elemental Body communicates directly with the soul, the Higher Self. However, as noted in previous chapters, the Middle Self (Human Consciousness) needs to communicate with the Higher Self through the body. This brings us to Adam, who in our tale represents Human Consciousness.

As the story continues, Adam succumbs to the influence of the body, the Lower Self. This is reflected in Eve giving Adam a taste of the forbidden fruit. This "opens their eyes" and they discover they are naked, which means separated from the oneness of the "Garden" and therefore self-aware. In the tale they make aprons of fig leafs, a fruit associated in the Old Faith with initiation. The "couple" has indeed passed across the threshold.

At this point in the tale, God is strolling through the garden but cannot locate Adam, to whom it calls out: "Where are you?" In other words, the Higher Self extends its presence into the material world but cannot sense Human Consciousness. Adam replies that he is hiding because he is naked (in new awareness of his being). God asks how it is that he knows himself in this way now and presses Adam by asking if he has eaten the forbidden fruit. Adam answers yes, and then passes the responsibility to Eve (the Elemental Body). Eve is then questioned in the same manner and passes responsibility to the serpent. This represents the breakdown of communication and the associated disconnect between the Middle and Lower Selves when something blocks communication with the Higher Self.

We are left now with only one unexamined character in our story, and that is the serpent. Eve expresses that the serpent beguiled her, and that he is the reason she ate the forbidden fruit. When people see or hear the word "beguiled," they think of deception, which is actually only one meaning of it; the word can also simply mean to interest. In any case, Dr. Nehama Aschkenasy, a Hebrew scholar, points out that in Hebrew the word which is translated as "beguiled" in the Bible does not mean "tricked" or "deceived" as commonly accepted. Instead, Aschkenasy says that the Hebrew word is a rare verb that indicates an intense multilevel experience evoking great emotional, psychological, and/or spiritual trauma. In this light, the serpent was the catalyst that caused Eve to come into self-awareness, which then makes one turn her thoughts to purpose and personal role in existence. In the story, Eve says she desired the wisdom that eating the fruit offered, which again speaks to self-realization and what can follow from that state of being.

Let us return to the figure of the serpent in the myth of Eden. Who is he? In our scenario the serpent is the DNA, the original design, the yet unmanifested plan. In the story, Adam and Eve have no genetic parents, and so we can view them as simply representing pure consciousness. Eve, as the Elemental Body still in its purity as energy, is presented with the idea of material manifestation and the power of lineage that is possible through what the serpent offers. She can become manifest, and through her as a body, a spiritual process can flow into material existence.

In our story we see the theme in which the Elemental Body is coaxed into formation when the Ancestors and the soul envision reincarnation. Prior to that event the Elemental Body is more potential than it is anything manifest. It must respond to the invitation of the serpent; it must accept it and become a vessel that can grow "wise"—that is, it can evolve through self-awareness and realization.

The story of Eden ends with God informing Eve that as a consequence of her actions, her desire will now be for her husband, and that he will rule over her. What we can see in this (instead of gender assignments) is the role between the Elemental Body and Human Consciousness. It is perhaps best reflected in view of the Hawaiian Kahuna that the Unihipilli (the so-called Lower Self) loves and is completely devoted to the Uhane (the so-called Middle Self). It is described as wanting to please Uhane in everyway. The soul establishes this relationship for the purpose of communication and the evolution of both the Lower and Middle Selves. Therefore we can see "God" in the Eden tale as the soul assigning roles to consciousness, but not out of punishment. The three are brought into unification and functionality. The idea is not to stay happily inert within an enclosed garden, no matter how lovely or perfect it is, but to instead become one's full potentiality.

Serpent in the Shadowed Places

In contrast to the depiction of the serpent as the Cosmic Life Force, we also find it connected to Underworld themes. In such cases there is typically an element of prophecy connected in one way or another. One example is the python associated with the Oracle at Delphi in ancient Greece. According to the old tales, the goddess Gaia kept a holy or sacred serpent in a chasm beneath the earth, from which vapors drifted upward. A shepherd happened upon the chasm and experienced the onset of prophetic abilities. Others followed in time and had similar experiences. The entire myth changes later on with the tale of Apollo slaying the python. This alters the theme and creates the idea that fumes from the rotting corpse of the great python bestow the gift of prophecy. A temple to Apollo was erected at the site and the cult featured a priestess who sat upon a tripod set over the chasm; here she breathed in the rising fumes and revealed the future. Of interest is the design of the three-legged tripod associated with altered states of consciousness. We do not seem to be able to separate ourselves from the number three when it comes to the mystical.

In the system at Delphi, we can see the repetitive theme we have been working with in this book. The fumes from the serpent represent the Elemental Body influencing Human Consciousness. The spiritual or "soul" element is present in the setting being the Temple of Apollo, and so we see the coming together again of body, mind, and soul. The primary difference here is that communication is not directed upward to the Higher Self above Human Consciousness, but is expressed outward through the latter into the material world. It is the serpent speaking through a human vessel and is therefore communication of the sacred DNA of the Great Python. This makes it Ancestral in nature. In other words, it is the Ancestors speaking from the Underworld.

This idea connects us to another that is sometimes called Shadow or the Organic Memory of the Earth. We touched upon this in Chapter Two. Shadow holds the memory of all life energy, which is absorbed at death and through the process of decomposition. Shadow can be thought of as the Lower Self of the earth's body where memory is retained on the "cellular level." Just as the human body has memory, so too does the body of our planet.

The level of serpent communication suggested by the Oracle at Delphi speaks to very deep and primal areas of our Elemental Consciousness. This is the serpent as reptilian and being the complete opposite of Human Consciousness. It is Human

Consciousness/Middle Self giving over to the Elemental Body/ Lower Self. Here communication becomes unconscious and we are propelled by an inner knowing that is beyond the reach of a conscious knowing. It is untraceable personal gnosis because it rises from the non-linear within the subconscious mind. This is the language that shamans refer to as "language-twisting-twisting" or more simply as "twisted language." Jeremy Narby touches on this in his book *The Cosmic Serpent*.

The approach of twisted language is to call common things by other names. To use the common name is to stay fixed on all that is taught and associated with it. We are, in effect, too close to the commonly named thing; only by calling it something else can we step back far enough away to see it as a whole instead of its finite nature. It is the language of dreams as well as the shifting images within the dream state. In a dream you can pick up a rifle and have it turn into a rake. This makes no sense to the conscious mind in the moment because it is not the language of the waking consciousness. The meaning is in the shift, and the object is only a means to reach the message.

Throughout the dream state the serpent slowly slithers, directing us as the dream unfolds. While it is the soul that is communicating to Human Consciousness within a dream, the serpent works with it to bind us to the experience and carry that back to us in the waking state. Whether the dream is pleasant or a nightmare depends upon how we embrace or reject what the serpent's whispers offer us from the branches of the Ancestral tree.

In the shadowed places of the mind it is easy to misinterpret the ways of the serpent, and this typically results in its vilification. For example, in the myth of the giant ash tree known as Yggdrasil a serpent is depicted as gnawing away at the deepest root in order to topple the tree. The falling of the tree is prophesized as the end of the world. However the end of one thing is the beginning of another. Let us look deeper into the work of this serpent.

The serpent associated with Yggdrasil is called Nidhogg. He is found beneath the tree in the zone of Niflheim, which contains the realm of the Dead. In addition to trying to gnaw through the root of the tree, Nidhogg also feeds on the bodies of dead corpses; these lay on what is called the corpse shore. Mircea Eliade, professor of Religious History, writes: "Because snakes are lunar—that is eternal—and live underground, embodying (among many other things) the souls of the dead, they know all secrets, are the source of all wisdom, and can foresee the future." In this light the serpent consumes the Dead, digesting all their experiences in life. Here it is the DNA flowing back into the Ancestral Spirit. The Dead in Niflheim are those who lived life poorly and in bad ways. This connects us back to theme of Ancestral redemption. New Elemental bodies will be generated by the Cosmic Serpent through Ancestral lineage in hopes of finding a champion to redeem the misdeeds.

At the bottom of the root in Niflheim there is a spring or a well known as Hvergelmir. I have seen this name translated as both "bubbling, boiling spring" and "bubbling cauldron." In either case, it is said that many rivers flow from it into the Nine Worlds that hang on Yggdrasil. We can look at this as the many rivers of blood that flow through various lineage lines across time from generation to generation.

In the myth of Yggdrasil, three figures known as the Norns draw water from the Well of Urd and pour it out on the gnawed root. This restores the root back to normal, which can be viewed as the process whereby the DNA structure is kept from morphing and losing its integrity. The Well of Urd contains, in essence, the waters of destiny and the three Norns (there is that number again) are the Fates. In the use of "destiny" to restore the root we can see the plan or design needs to stay uncorrupted, the DNA must be preserved. What "is to be" is kept hydrated by the waters of destiny.

As the myth continues, we find that in the end the serpent succeeds in gnawing through the root. He then gathers the Dead with him and ascends up to the very realm of the gods. Here we can see the theme of the evolution of consciousness, the Elemental Body rising from the Ancestral Realm, transcending its lower abode and entering into a higher realm or state of consciousness. The "end of the world" is the end of one finite phase of reality and the birth of a new higher order.

Another type of serpent that can be assigned to "the shadowed places" is the guardian snake. This is not to be confused with the guardian dragon in Western culture, for the dragon guards things he has no personal use for, such as a treasure of gold or gems and young virgin maidens, whereas the snake guards things not intended for the average person such as special portals and most particularly trees or the fruit that grows on them. Guardian serpents are also associated with rites of initiation. Noteworthy in myth and legend is the offering of honey cakes to guardian serpents, and as mentioned earlier, there is a connection between bees, the Dead, and the realm of the Ancestral Spirit.

In the myth of the Garden of the Hesperides we find some interesting features we can connect to the Ancestral theme and a guardian serpent. The legendary garden was located in the West, which is the gateway to the realm of the Dead. The garden was tended by three women called the Hesperides; they were also known as the Nymphs of Sunset, and the Evening

Daughters of Night. In the center of their garden was an apple tree bearing golden apples; this fruit granted immortality.

The apple tree was guarded by a serpent with a hundred heads who was known as Ladon (he is also known as the Hesperian Dragon). In the myth, Ladon is slain by Hercules, who is a demigod (half-Human and half-Divine). In this we can see our figures of Human Consciousness and Soul Consciousness jointly holding power over the Elemental Body. In other words, we are Hercules when the three act as one. The apples represent the Divine fruition of achievable consciousness. The serpent is withholding access to the immortality of the individual, and we can regard this as the limitations of the flesh body. In other words, the inevitable fate of the body is to die. If we are nothing but the body, then this finality is our fate as well. However, the hero Hercules is ultimately successful in obtaining the fruit of immortality, which we can regard as Human Consciousness (when hand-in-hand with Soul Consciousness) has the ability to conquer the cycle of life and death in the Material Realm.

The serpent is the guardian and the liberator. What seems sinister about the serpent is actually what we fear from within our emotional makeup. The snake is reptilian, seemingly unemotional and coldly logical. It reminds us of our weaknesses and imperfections; it reminds us that we can make the wrong choices when our emotions and fears enter into our reasoning.

Unlike the hero in Western mythology we are not to slay the guardian serpent in order to complete our quest. Instead we are to hear its ancient Ancestral tales, listen to its rooted wisdom, and uncover what is hidden from us that keeps us contained in ignorance. With the serpent, the Spirit-Rider, carried on our back, the Ancestral Eye can lend added vision on our quest.

CHAPTER 7

The Starry Path
of the Round

In this chapter we will tie some things together from other chapters, and we will look deeper into the idea of the old Ancestral gods. These old stories are important for two reasons. The first reason is that they preserve a mindset if not an actual history. Mindsets are important because they connect firmly with the currents or streams upon which they firmly draw. The greater importance is not whether we are looking at memory or perception; the importance is what rises in our spirit because of these tales.

The second important reason is that what we stay connected with is what draws that person, place, or thing deeper into our lives and inner spirits. Through mind, body, and soul we build and maintain bridges of thought, emotion, and longing. There is a metaphysical principle that states "like attracts like." This means that we attract to ourselves the things that resonate with our personal energy vibration. That is both good news and bad news. The conditions of our lives are reflections of this active principle, and it reveals our heart (in light or darkness). Does your heart include or exclude?

By studying the stellar-based lore of our origins we draw closer to the principles and energies they hold for us. We can follow the energy trail across time and become bearers of it ourselves. Within us we carry the flame passed to us from our creators. It forges the mind, body, and spirit. It is, in essence, a circulating flame that lights the way from origin, to life, to death, and to rebirth. Its flickering light is a promise of return to the stars. We need only let it burn within and shine without.

Throughout this book we have looked at the model of the Three Selves. We have seen the Elemental Body, which is produced through the actions of the Four Elements. The earliest mention of them in Western literature depicts them as existing in space, what we can now call the place of the stars. The soul has been presented as originating amidst the stars. We explored the concept of Human Consciousness and noted that it resides and operates within a body made from star dust. Now we must integrate this knowledge and change it into realization. We must work with it to achieve that goal. The chapter on connection through ritual will help you map this out.

To further review, in the book we noted an Ancestral myth in which the "old gods" or "first gods" came from the stars. They passed a "spirit of consciousness" to our Ancestors who, in turn, have passed it to descendants across the ages. One image for this transmission is the serpent. We explored it from the idea of ancient Ancestral veneration, to the double helix snake-like formation of our DNA, to the depiction of the Spirit-Rider. This last is sent in serpent form by the Ancestral Spirit and attaches itself to a descendant. Are you willing to invite this into your life? Would you share the Ancestral Eye?

The symbol of the serpent is powerful and extremely ancient. Its first appearance is in the old tales of the Cosmic Serpent. This conceptual being, or one related to it, appears to be a universal one well-rooted in Ancient cultures across the earth. It entered into their myths and legends, and left its mark in the stars (through constellations). Ancient Egyptian culture is rich in the serpent concept, and the Universe is often depicted as a serpent devouring the sun. This is not unlike the imagery of the Ouroboros in which a serpent swallows its own tail. This represents the perpetual, cyclic renewal of repeating cycles.

The Ouroboros also represents the eternal return, the cycle of life, death, and rebirth, leading to immortality. In an earlier chapter we noted the Garden of the Hesperides in which grew a tree that produced fruit granting immortality. It was guarded by a serpent, and in one myth this serpent was cast into the night sky and became the constellation of Dracos. There it guards the greater fruit of immortality found in the Grove of Stars. Are you willing to reach upward towards the stars?

Serpent imagery is attached to the ancient concept of the axis mundi when the latter is seen as a tree. The axis mundi is the center where the heavens meet the earth. In tree form its branches touch the sky, its trunk meets the earth, and its roots reach down into the Underworld. Of side interest is the fact that in old Polynesian cultures we find the belief that Ancestral spirits reside in a banyan tree. One variety of the banyan is the bodhi tree (beneath which Buddha became enlightened). In these old views we can see the importance of the Tree of the Ancestors: the Tree of Voices, the Tree of Souls. Do you know where your axis mundi exists? Will you sit there receptively for as long as it takes to hear the voices of those who came before you?

In ancient Mayan religion we find a mysterious figure known as the Vision Serpent. It sits atop the World Tree. The Mayans called on it in bloodletting rituals to bring the Ancestors up from the Underworld and back down from the heavens. Priests would then commune with them for various needs and purposes. Here we see this serpent as a direct link between the realms of spiritkind and humankind. The Vision Serpent was evoked by dripping blood from a pierced tongue or genitals onto bark paper. The paper was then burned, and the Vision Serpent emerged from the rising smoke. What would you offer or withhold from a Vision Serpent?

In imagery the Vision Serpent is depicted with an Ancestor or a god emerging from its open mouth. This is strongly reminiscent of the Spirit-Rider carrying the Ancestral Eye in its mouth. The Vision Serpent establishes communication between the material and non-material planes. Here the serpent serves as a type of doorway through which we can access the Ancestral Spirit experience and integrate it into our material lives. It is a joining of body and mind.

Serpent symbolism also shows up in the concept of the Kundalini, which is attached to mystical systems in India. The word comes from the Sanskrit meaning "coiled one" and is therefore most often depicted in art as a serpent. Kundalini is thought of as a vital energy residing at the base of the human spine. It has the power to bestow enlightenment when raised upward into the conscious mind. The seat of the Kundalini is in the "tailbone" of the human body, which in anatomy is called the sacrum. This name is derived from the Latin *sacer*, which means "sacred."

The sacrum is a triangular bone made up of five fused vertebrae. In this we see the mystical number three again (three tips of the triangle) and the five elements of Greek philosophy: air, fire, water, earth, and spirit. The theme of the sacrum ties in nicely with the Kahuna concept of an etheric tail extending from the Elemental Body (noted in an earlier chapter).

In the Kundalini practice the goal is to raise the serpent energy (known also as the serpent fire) up and into the pineal gland, which is located in the area of the forehead. In mystical systems this is known as the Third Eye or Psychic Eye. Once this area is empowered, it is believed to bestow expanded awareness and "Otherworld" vision. It is interesting to note that the ancient headdress of an Egyptian pharaoh sported a serpent's head facing out from the forehead area.

A pharaoh was both a ruler and religious figure in ancient Egypt. He bore the titles Lord of the Two Lands and High Priest of All Temples. The former title referred to his rulership over upper and lower Egypt. In this we can see a connection to Human Consciousness over the Elemental Body. In the pharaoh's title of High Priest of All Temples we can see a connection to the indwelling soul in the human body.

In mystical thought, two currents of energy flow from the sacrum to the pineal gland. The common names for these currents are the Ida and the Pingala. They form an elongated vertical "figure-eight" with the lines intersecting at the solar plexus and meeting again at the brow area (although in some systems they are envisioned as meeting at the nostrils). From a metaphysical perspective the currents are electrical and magnetic energies. In appearance they resemble the entwined serpents on a caduceus, which is a staff carried by the god Hermes (who we encountered in an earlier chapter addressing his nature as an escort of the Dead). We also noted that among the earliest depictions in art, Hermes wears a black cloth covered with stars. Would you work to evoke the inner flame and awaken in the starry heavens?

In imagery the Ida current is assigned to the left side of the body, and the Pingala to the right side. The Ida is considered feminine and given the color white in its symbolism. The

Pingala is considered masculine and assigned the color red. They climb the spine like the serpents on the caduceus, and in this light we can view the spine as a type of inner World Tree, our internal axis mundi.

In mystical cosmology a series of seven chakra centers are assigned to the spine. They represent the upper and lower worlds, and the spine is the axis of being. Each chakra is a portal into these worlds (or regions of consciousness). Flowing in and out of them, the Pingala brings to consciousness critical and analytical reasoning; it bears the title of the Sun Force. Ida brings to consciousness that which is conceptual and creative in nature; it bears the title Moon Force. Moving through them (under certain circumstances) is the serpent fire, the Kundalini force.

When activated the Kundalini ascends upward through the channel provided by the Ida and Pingala. The serpent fire then coils in the brow center where it affects an altered state of consciousness. Afterwards it descends back to its den into the sacrum, where it awaits the return of the environment that will summon it once again.

In Kundalini yoga, the use of breath is extremely vital to the desired outcome. As noted in earlier chapters the connection between the breath and the Ancestors is vital to continuance and communication between the generations. The serpent fire is empowered by the flame passed to us by the Ancestral gods. It is ancient star fire given to us by the old gods who came from the stars.

Star Gods

Our distant Ancestors brought forth the testimonials of the old gods in a way we cannot do today, for they knew more about them than anyone who came afterwards. History became myth and myth became legend (to borrow a line from the *Lord of the Rings* movie). We stand now divided with an academic book in one hand and the Ancestral Eye in the other. How then do we shape our vision?

The ancient Greek writings offer us a valuable record of old beliefs because they are among the oldest writings we have in Western culture. Scholars such as Plato envision that the Universe came into being through the action of a Divine Source, a Divine Consciousness. One model depicts the creation of the World Soul as being the first to manifest. Ancient thought later divided it into three sections: the region of the fixed stars; Middle Space containing the planets, sun, and moon; and lastly the Region of Earth.

Divine Consciousness (Source of All Things) did not want to create earthly beings (mortals) itself because it did not want them to be equal to what created them. The idea here is that the essential spirit of the creator passes into his or her creation. So the Source created a race of sidereal beings, the so-called star gods. The bodies of these gods were, for the most part, composed of fire.

The Source entrusted the star gods with "the intelligent embryos of souls" and instructed them to add a corruptible nature to living beings. In this way humankind was fashioned from the substance of the World Soul, and the star gods became the caretakers and guardians of their creation—human beings. Into the creation of humankind, the star gods added the three intellectual capacities: opinion, knowledge, and contemplation. In a later time the Mystery Traditions were formed by a small segment of humans, and in these traditions an important phrase arose, which may well be a remnant memory of the first Ancestors: "Though I am born of the earth, my race is of the starry skies."

It is the "corruptible nature" of humankind that leads us to work death into the theme of the star people. In old cultures (such as those of South, Central, and North America) that remained living closer to Nature than did European ones, we find a strong Afterlife connection to the stars of the Milky Way. Myths and old lore of these regions call the Milky Way by related names such as the Pathway of the Departed, the Ghost Road, and the Spirit Road. It is depicted as a path or road to the Otherworld, and is traveled by spirits and deities (as well as by shamans in a state of trance).

A common theme related to the path of the Milky Way is that of the Guardian at the Entrance. In some of the tales, souls are turned back and have to return to the earth. This is not, however, the same spirit we find in religions such as Christianity that see some souls as unworthy or tainted beyond redemption. The Guardians, in the old ways, turn back souls who are not prepared to enter. These souls are sent back to become prepared and not to be forever denied entry. It is an old story from a time before the solar god came to displace the star god.

We can continue our exploration of the star gods by turning to what we know of the old gods known as the Titans. They are said to descend from the primordial or primal gods that were born out of Chaos. For the purposes of this chapter we will focus on a god known as Astraios, whose name means "The Starry One." He was the father of the Four Winds' minor gods called Boreas, Eurus, Notus, and Zephyrus. Astraios also had a son with the goddess Eos, who was named Hesperus. The son was associated with the evening star (the planet Venus) and he fathered the Hesperides (Guardians of the Apples of Immortality).

These deities appear to form an original cast directly connected to the origins and conditions of the first humans. In them we see the continuing themes of fire and breath, the latter represented by the Four Winds. The stars, thought of as flickering flames, remain constant in the tales of the star gods.

Our story continues with the coming of the Olympian gods who were born from the Titans. In time a challenge, a war, erupted between the Titans and the Olympians. The Titans were defeated, and with the establishment of the Olympians as the ruling gods, written history begins among the ancient Greeks. The Olympians create a realm on top of Mount Olympus, which can be seen to represent a significant establishment of the axis mundi within ancient Greek culture.

In the Greek (and Roman) myths that pertain to the theme in this chapter, we find the gods turn various people, animals, and creatures into stars. In most cases this is done to honor their memory or to remove them from the earth. In a few cases it is regarded as deifying, setting one among the stars. However, there is another way to look at this theme, and it is one of returning a person back to his or her original essence—the substance of stars.

In the cast of star beings that intervene in the human race we find the race known as the Irin or the Watchers. They appear in esoteric writings such the Book of Enoch. Enoch depicts them as "angels," but I view this depiction as the diminishment of the star god theme over the ages (coupled with the suppression of the conquered cultures by their conquerors). To diminish the old gods lifts up the new ones (or the One) that have come to displace what lived in the before time.

Tracking the changing stories is important to understanding what changes took place and where things are now. It is not unlike understanding changes in family, why some moved away, how communication is or isn't working, and what if anything we can or should do about it. In this light let us follow the journey of the star people known as the Watchers.

We can look at the old, the stellar mythos, and interpret the Watchers as an old race of star gods who guarded the heavens and the earth. Their nature, as well as their "rank," was altered by the successive Lunar and Solar Cults that displaced the earlier Stellar Cults. In time the Greeks reduced the Watchers to being spirits of the four winds, followed by the Christians who further diminished them to principalities of the air. Still, we can see the remaining core connection to the star god Astraios and his offspring as ancient star gods.

Mystic Cabalists organized the Watchers into Archangels, which I assume are derived from the early Hebrew concept of an order of angels known as the Irin. According to this doctrine the Irin were ruled over by four great angels known as Michael, Gabriel, Raphael, and Auriel. It seems likely that the Hebrews borrowed (and then altered) this entire concept from the surrounding cultures they mixed with, which were stellar and lunar in nature.

In many modern systems these ancient beings are the Guardians of the Dimensional Planes, protectors of the ritual circle, and witnesses to the rites that are said to have been kept down through the ages. Each of the ruling Watchers oversees a "Watchtower," which is now a portal marking one of the four quarters of the ritual circle. Interesting side note: In days of old, a "tower" was a military fighting unit, and a "watchtower" was a defending home unit, similar to a National Guard.

Outside of the modern structure, the Watchers are most easily linked to the concept of "guardian angels." In the Old Testament (Daniel 4:13–17) there is reference made to the

Irin, which appear to be an order of angels (in early Hebrew lore the Irin were a high order of angels who sat on the supreme Judgment Council of the Heavenly Court). In the *Apocryphal Books of Enoch and Jubilees*, the Watchers are mentioned as Fallen Angels who originally were sent to earth to teach men law and justice. In the *Secret Book of Enoch*, the Watchers are listed as rebellious angels who followed Sataniel in a heavenly war.

Gustav Davidson, in his *Dictionary of Angels*, portrays the Watchers as a high order of angels. In Rabbinic and Cabalistic lore, the "good" Watchers dwell in the 5th Heaven, and "evil" Watchers dwell in the 3rd Heaven. The Watchers of the 5th Heaven are ruled over by the archangels Uriel, Raphael, Michael, and Gabriel. In the *Apocryphon of Genesis*, it is said that Noah is the offspring of a Watcher who slept with Bat-Enosh, his mother.

In the *Dictionary of Angels*, the Watchers are listed as the Fallen Angels who instructed humankind in the ancient arts. The most common associations found in various texts on medieval magic regarding the Watchers are as follows:

1. Araqiel: taught the signs of the earth
2. Armaros: taught the resolving of enchantments
3. Azazel: taught the art of cosmetics
4. Barqel: taught astrology
5. Ezequeel: taught the knowledge of the clouds
6. Gadreel: taught the making of weapons of war
7. Kokabeel: taught the mystery of the Stars
8. Penemue: taught writing
9. Sariel: taught the knowledge of the Moon
10. Semjaza: taught Herbal enchantments
11. Shamshiel: taught the signs of the Sun

It is these same angels who are referred to as the Sons of God in the Book of Genesis who mated with human women. According to Christian mythology their "sins" filled the earth with violence and the world was destroyed as a result of their intervention. Read Genesis 6:1–7 for the background in biblical reference.

Richard Cavendish, in his book *The Powers of Evil*, makes references to the possibilities of the Giants mentioned in Genesis 6:4 being the Giants or Titans of Greek mythology. He also lists the Watchers as the Fallen Angels that magicians call forth in ceremonial magic. Cavendish draws some interesting parallels and even mentions that the Watchers were so named because they were stars, the "eyes of night," which can be regarded easily as a reference to the stars.

Saint Paul, in the New Testament, calls the Fallen Angels "principalities": "for we are not contending against flesh and blood, but against the principalities, against the powers . . . against the spiritual hosts of wickedness in High Places." It was also Saint Paul who titled the biblical figure of Satan "the prince of power of the air." Christian theologians promote the notion that Satan is connected to "a star" by interpreting the Book of Isaiah 14:12–14 as referring to him as fallen from the heights—heaven. The verses actually address the King of Babylon, but theologians argue that the passages are metaphors for Satan.

The 16th-century French theologian named Sinistrari spoke of Beings existing between Humans and Angels. He called them Demons, and associated them with the Elemental natures of Earth, Air, Fire, and Water. This, however, was not a new concept but was taught by certain gnostic sects in the early days of Christianity. However, there was (and is) a difference between the rooted ideas of a daemon in Greek thought as opposed to a demon in Christian views. The former was an intelligence of a natural order of beings, whereas a demon was depicted as a creature of chaos.

Clement of Alexandria, influenced by Hellenistic cosmology, attributed the movement of the stars and the control of the Four Elements to angelic beings. Sinistrari attributed bodies of fire, air, earth, and water to these beings, and concluded that the Watchers were made of fire and air. Cardinal Newman, writing in the mid-1800s, proposed that certain angels existed who were neither totally good nor evil, and had only "partially fallen" from the heavens. This would seem to support Davidson's text which places the Watchers in two different "heavens."

Many modern systems view the Watchers as Elemental Rulers, "lords" of the Four Elements of Creation: Earth, Air, Fire, and Water. In metaphysics these forces are believed to be empowered by spiritual creatures known as Elementals. Old traditions assign folkloric beings to the Elements to symbolize their active principle. In this assignment we have gnomes in the element of Earth; within Air, the Sylphs; within Fire, the Salamanders; and within Water, the Undines. In traditional lore these Elemental races each have their own ruler, and so for Earth it is Gob; for Air, Paralda; for Fire, Djin; and for Water, Necksa.

This is the state of arrival in which we find the Watchers today. An alternative view is to see them as those who watch the generations pass into one another. They lend their vision to the Ancestral Spirit in which the Ancestors act to send "agents" aid or correct the current as it moves towards the manifestation of another generation.

You can choose to work with the Watchers in accord with your view. In the lore of the Watchers they came to aid humans by teaching them advancements. We saw this as a list of eleven things they introduced into human society. Our Ancestors took this knowledge and adapted it, not always for the best results. If you are interested in working with them you can find ritual material in books on Wicca and ceremonial magic.

Reaching for a Star

When speaking of the stars or starry realms, it is almost impossible not to include the Faery or Elven race. This is not because they are "star beings" in the conventional sense of the term, but because there is a connective lore. Sometimes they are referred to as being in or of starry light. In most cases this is a depiction of the illuminated form of their bodies or what surrounds their bodies.

A direct connection between stars and the "Elven" race is found in the mythos created by J.R.R. Tolkien (and offshoots of it). Although the mythos that we see in his *Lord of the Rings* stories are not the accepted myths of known cultures, they do essentially come from the same place—the human spirit. Myths speak to us in a language that bypasses history and is understood by something greater than human reasoning. They are not true and they are not false; they exist in-between fact and fiction (which is the most magical of all places). In this light, the mythos that Tolkien left us is no less valid or authentic than the myths of the Greeks, Celts, Norse, or any other people.

In Tolkien's mythos we find a hero figure known as Eärendil who is depicted as a seafarer. In one tale he carries a star (or the light of a star) across the sea. This is sometimes referred to as the Star of Eärendil, the most beloved star of the Elven race (to borrow a line from the *Lord of the Rings* movie). The mythos involves crystals known as the silmarils or silmarilli. These crystals were fashioned from the essence of the Two Trees of Valinor (also known as the Trees of the Valar). One tree was called Laurelin (the gold tree) and the other was called Telerion (the silver tree). It is noteworthy to reflect back upon the Silver Bough of Northern European lore, and the Golden Bough of Southern European lore.

As the mythos goes, the trees were destroyed but not before the Valar took their last flower and fruit, which were then made into the sun and moon. While the sun is a star, the moon is not. The Star of Eärendil seems to not be either, but is instead Venus, the evening star. According to a letter written in 1967, Tolkien credited the origin of *Eärendil* to the Anglo-Saxon word *earendel*, which he interpreted as Venus (the morning and the evening star). In this light we can regard the Star of Eärendil as being the light of Venus captured in one of the crystals fashioned by Fëanor, the great craftsman and gemsmith of the Elves. This idea seemingly departs from the formal Tolkien mythos that mentions only Laurelin and Telperion. However, in Tolkien's story *The Voyage of Eärendil* (written around 1914 and later retitled *The Last Voyage of Eärendil*) there is reason to conclude that the star is Venus. This is connected to the ecliptic path of the Moon and Venus, which gives us the distinction we need in this matter.

From the misty pre-origins of myths we find the star and faery surfacing in the imaginations of various writers and poets. One modern depiction is the Blue Faery in the tale of Pinocchio. In this mythos she holds a wand mounted by a star, and we find this in many modern fairytales. Of special interest is fairytale author Christine Messina's mention that Cinderella's faery helper is actually the spirit of her dead mother returned to aid her. This speaks to the theme of faeries being associated with the spirit of the Dead, and by extension to the stars (in the theme of reincarnation).

A popular image in contemporary lore is what is commonly called the "Faery Star" or Septagram (seven-pointed star). It is also sometimes called the Elvenstar, which I prefer and will use as this chapter continues. For me this star represents the spirit of what is conveyed in myth and legend. It is pre-belief and pre-history. It comes from the fount of inner knowing, what is passed in the flame of the Ancestral gods. We are heirs to the star tales, the star lore of another reality.

In modern views the Faery Star is regarded as a gift from faeries to humans to bridge the understanding between the two realms. It is thought of as a gateway symbol, a portal or entrance between our world and that of Faery, the Otherworld. As such, modern practitioners assign various aspects to each tip of the star. These comprise a list of spiritual and mental attributes.

For the purposes of this chapter we will work with the seven points as representing the pathways here on the Earth Plane. Each point represents a link and an alignment to the Otherworld. The star also symbolizes the seven directions: north, east, south, west, above, below, and in-between. In some modern traditions the star symbolizes Earth, Air, Fire, Water, Mind, Body, and Spirit.

In this chapter, as a symbol, each point on the Elvenstar signifies a connective allocation related to its connection to material reality. Beginning at the top and moving clockwise the points represent: sun, magic, wind, moon, door, woods, and sea. When used in meditation and magic, the symbol is traced out in an unbroken line. This changes the order of the point assignments as indicated in the illustration: sun, moon, sea, wind, woods, magic, door. This is not a problem if you retain alignment to the star points (the alignment exercise is provided later in the chapter).

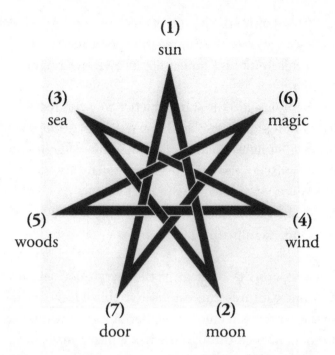

(1)
sun

(3)
sea

(6)
magic

(5)
woods

(4)
wind

(7)
door

(2)
moon

The core essence of the teachings surrounding the Elvenstar involves the presence and emanation of light and how it flows to us for practical purposes. The sun, which is actually a star, symbolizes the higher light emanation. This light represents spirit, and therefore light and spirit become one and the same in the Elvenstar teachings.

The metaphorical teachings depict light emanating from a higher plane (star point one) and channeled into the mortal world (star point two). The light of the moon is reflected into the Mortal Realm by the sea and given force in the tides (star point three). The wind arises from the tides and carries the light across the realm of mortalkind (star point four).

The trees catch the light on the breeze and gather it for those who seek enlightenment (star point five). The light resides within the trees and awaits the awakening, which is magic (star point six). Magic opens the doorway or portal that allows access to the Source (star point seven).

Each star point assignment has its own elven significance:

1. Sun: signifies the star or higher consciousness
2. Moon: signifies enlightenment within the darkness
3. Sea: signifies the reflection and force of light
4. Wind: signifies the movement of light
5. Woods: signifies attachment to the light
6. Magic: signifies alignment with the light
7. Door: signifies passage to the source

In ancient lore the concept of the faery door set within a tree trunk captures the essence of this Elvenstar theme. Here the symbolism comes together binding the light of sun and moon, filtered through the trees, into a magical setting through which an altered state of consciousness can be attained. Such an attainment allows one to enter into another dimension of time and space.

The Elvenstar Alignment

Needed items:

Elvenstar image

1 forest green candle

1 herbal sprig (a pinch of any live herb)

Seeds (grain, rice, or a seed packet)

1 charm (a leaf or stone)

1 small key

1 piece of cord

1 white poster board with marker

For this exercise/technique you will need to use a posterboard on which you will draw a large triangle. On each tip of the triangle you will draw a circle about two inches in diameter. In the top circle of the triangle you will place the green candle. Attach the herbal sprig with a string, binding it to the shaft of the candle.

In the lower right circle place the seeds. In the lower left circle place the charm. In the center of the triangle place the cord attached to the small key.

The underlying purpose of this rite is to deepen rapport with the Old Ones of the primal forces. Throughout the chapters of this book you have been introduced to the concept of other beings that dwell outside of our physical existence. Now it is time to open the inner gateway and move further along the pathways.

Before you begin, pick up the Elvenstar and trace the pattern with a fingertip:

1. Sun: Touch the top point of the star with your left index finger. This point is a sign of the sacred source that exists outside and within all things.
2. Moon: Slide your finger down to this point, following the line down in an unbroken path. This is a sign of the light in the places of darkness, which signifies enlightenment within the darkness.
3. Sea: Move your finger up to this point. This is a sign of light reflected from within, and then outward to others.
4. Wind: Now you move your finger along the line to this point. This is a sign of the light carried into the world and across all barriers.
5. Woods: Move your finger across to this point. This is a sign of sacred space, the point in time and space where veneration and alignment are freely offered.

6. Magic: Move your finger upward to the next point. This point is a sign of shaped reality, the power of mind and spirit over material manifestation.

7. Door: Move your finger down to the next point. This point is a sign of passage, a crossing to and a crossing from. It is the access point and the moment of interface with that which is greater than the self. As a last gesture, you move your finger back up to the top point, which reunites one with the source.

Spend a few moments thinking about the Divine spirit permeating Nature, and reflect upon the links symbolized by the Elvenstar. The sun and moon symbolize the masculine and feminine forms that represent the Divine Source. The sea is the life essence of the very tides of existence. The wind is the presence and activity of spirit within the material world. The trees are the sacred groves, the wind catchers that hold sacred space. Magic is the mutable nature of the energy gifted to us by Divinity. The door is the act of accepting and entering into the mysteries that lie beyond our current level of understanding.

Following your meditation on the Elvenstar, set the Elvenstar symbol down near the base of the triangle of circles. Now light the candle in the top circle, and placing the palms of your hands towards the candle, say:

> "Light in the places of darkness,
> three are the things that bless.
> (Pause.)
> Eyes to see the nights and days,
> to so be one with Elder Ways."
> (Reflect for a few moments upon the idea that you must be the light bearer who finds your truth within.)

Place your palms facing the left lower sphere containing your charm piece. Say these words:

"Spirit to body, to learn and rest,
three are the things that here do bless.
(Pause.)
Formed to know the nights and days,
and join me so to Elder Ways."

(Reflect for a few moments on the idea that spirits/souls enter into the Material Plane, and that you are one yourself, and that there are other spirits who are different and serve to aid you in your understanding and exploration of this life experience.)

Place your palms facing the lower right sphere containing the seeds. Say these words:

"Flower to seed, to pass the test,
three are the things that here do bless.
(Pause.)
Contained within the nights and days,
roots and growth for Elder Ways."

(Reflect for a few moments on the idea that all you do in life generates a ripple of energy, and think about what you want your energy to contribute to the world in which you and your loved ones now dwell.)

Now, place your palms facing the center of the triangle that contains the cord and key. Say these words:

"Key to open, the way to press,
three are the things that here do bless.
(Pause.)
Turning both the nights and days,
into the gates of Elder Ways."

(Reflect for a few moments on the idea that seeking is an energy, and that finding is the result, and that you do not walk alone. Instead, all who have come before you now guide you along on your own journey.)

When you feel ready to finish, take up the items and put everything away. You can add the charm, the star, and other items to a charm bag that you can carry with you to stay within the emanation of this energy. Keep the candle and use it again to repeat the alignment at a later time.

The Elvenstar Mental Journey

The purpose of this technique is to come into communication with an elven/faery being on the inner planes through a guided imagery journey. The journey provided here will supply you with basics for first contact.

You may wish to record the following journey on a tape recorder, or have someone do this for you in their voice. Read slowly with a brief pause between each sentence. The alignment is best performed on the night of the full moon, but you may perform this anytime during the waxing period. Before you begin the exercise, place the talisman in front of you.

(BEGIN TAPING) Imagine that you are standing at the crossroads in a remote woodland area. The moon lights the night sky and is filtered through the tree branches all around you. You remain at the crossroads for a few moments. A breeze softly drifts past you, and you can feel its touch.

In the distance you see a soft light, and it seems as though this might be a lantern moving in your direction. You silently watch the approaching light. It continues to slowly move in the darkness and towards the place where you stand.

As the light draws near, you begin to see that it is an illuminated figure. The light emanating from this being is as soft and bright as moonlight. The figure peacefully approaches you, and you gaze upon its features. It is an elven being from the Otherworld. The elven being speaks to you, and it has a message. Observe the being with your eyes of imagination and listen to it, speak with it.

(Leave about ten minutes of blank tape running, and then record the following alignment exercise).

The elven being hands you an Elvenstar talisman. Upon it you see a seven-pointed star etched into the talisman. You touch the top point of the star with your left index finger. This point is a sign of the sacred source that exists outside and within all things. It is the indwelling spark and the outdwelling presence that unites all things and maintains universal harmony.

You slide your finger down to the next point, following the line down in an unbroken path. This point is a sign of the light in the places of darkness, for here is the unconquerable light that cannot be overcome.

You move you finger up to the next point. This point is a sign of light reflected from within, and then outward to others. Now you move your finger along the line to the next point. This point is a sign of the light carried into the world and across all barriers.

You move your finger across to the next point. This point is a sign of sacred space, the point in time and space where veneration and alignment are freely offered. Next you move your finger upward to the next point. This point is a sign of shaped reality, the power of mind and spirit over material manifestation.

You move your finger down to the next point. This
point is a sign of passage, a crossing to and a crossing
from. It is the access point and the moment of inter-
face with that which is greater than the self. As a last
gesture, you move your finger back up to the top point,
which reunites one with the source. (END TAPING)

Spend a few moments looking at the Elvenstar image. When
not in use, place this in its protective wrappings. Whenever you
wish to interface with the Elven race, simply meditate on the
Elvenstar talisman for a few moments. Then perform the mental journey by returning to the crossroads and watching the elven being approach as in your original meditation. Be relaxed
and receptive, and do not force anything to happen. Just allow
it all to take place naturally as you remain open and receptive.
Keep a journal account of your experiences.

The Circle of Stars

The old star lore is connected to primordial and pre-human
eras. We can think of them as the pristine worlds, a time when
the Faery Realm had no borders with the realm of humankind.
The earth had clarity of mind in those days, unpopulated with
the toxins generated by human civilization. Our longing for a
"paradise" after death may be an inherited memory of the first
pure ages on the earth. Perhaps the tale of Adam and Eve in
the Garden of Eden is a marker of the state of consciousness in
which humans made a choice to leave the Old World in favor
of dominating all lands and things within them.

When humans first emerged as people, there were older races on earth. Their ways and traditions shaped our own over the
ages. Contact with these beings later on populated our stories
that are now relegated to myth, legend, and fairytale. Through

contact with other beings, and the way our Ancestors understood or misunderstood them, arose the seers and mystics of
the human race. Old tales tell of mating between faery or elven
and humans. This is also a theme connected to the star gods.

The idea that some humans have "mixed blood" in them
is a very old one. It was a popular theme back in the 1960s
and 1970s during which some people claimed to have faery
blood in them. Fewer claimed to have the blood of star gods
in them, but the knowledge of the old lore was not as well-
known then as it is now.

Do we look upon the stars simply for their beauty and
wonder? Or is this something of ancient memory within our
bodies and inner beings that stirs us? In the tradition that I
practice there are teachings that we are descended from the
stars. Our lives are guided through a spiritual quest that ultimately leads to a return to stars, a return to the Community
of Souls from which we came.

You and I stand beneath a circle of stars. It the beginning
and the conclusion, and we are placed in its very center. The
starry circle is not broken; it is a reminder that we are beings
within the natural order of things. This order is birth, life,
death, and renewal. It issues forth at the Source of All Things
and is embedded in all planes of existence.

The three-way crossroads awaits us all. In time there
will come to be a day when the Elemental Body, Human
Consciousness, and the Soul Body will all take different
roads. We walk the round here on Earth beneath the stars.
From the stars we look down to decide upon another round.
Stars make visions come true.

CHAPTER 8

Through the Gates of Evening

In current times many people bear deep wounds that are associated with family. Some of them are born of resentment, perceived wrongs, positions of injustice, and rejection. Many people from the gay, lesbian and transgendered community have shared their stories of family rejection, of being disowned by parents and siblings. This can make the idea of communing with the Ancestors feel undesirable. Unfortunately this cuts us off from the very source through which we can find liberation.

When we are mired in the brambles and quicksand of dysfunctional family dynamics and politics, the Ancestral flow almost comes to a standstill. This is not unlike a logjam in a river. Too many things have come together, and the will to resolve the situation becomes daunting. Some people choose to walk away, and some people choose to push away. It seems somehow safer to disengage, but the blood still links us to the same source.

If you place your fingers against a pulse point on your body, you can feel the Ancestors drumming to you across time. They drum to those in your family who hold ill will as well as to those who support you and stand with you. The drumbeat is equal. In this we can see that from a distance the vision is true and uncorrupted. We must bring this vision into our lives and make it real in the here and now. Part of this requires the dissolving away of fault.

In the Huna tradition we find the principle of "making things right." It is connected to the prayer and practice of what the Hawaiian Kahuna call Ho 'Oponopono. This practice is about dissolving blocks and filling in the resulting voids or vacuum with light. It is important to understand that making things right is sometimes an entirely solitary experience. It may not change other people in your life (or separated from your life) but it can make things right internally, deep within your own being.

When we make things right, the River of Blood spills over the banks and the current continues around the logjam. We become a tributary for its continuation. If you act from an inner place of knowing, a knowing that your life is what is right for you, then you have made things right. To be part of the logjam only feeds all that is contributing to each log's presence and contribution. In the chapter on "connective rites" you will find a ritual to help mend souls. This is an important tool for liberation.

In a previous section of this book we found the principle of "fault" and this functions as an energy connection known as the "aka cord." We noted that as long as one party holds fault, holds on to one end of the cord, both parties remain connected. This connection can continue after life has ended. It is this principle of fault that can draw us back into specific bloodlines as well as connect us in a next life with souls we knew in a previous one.

In a previous chapter we touched on the teachings of the astrological Star Gates and how advanced souls reincarnate. They return not for themselves but for others who can benefit from a soul incapable of holding an aka cord of fault. They offer liberation. As in all things, humans have a choice. They can choose teachings that are offered them as a means of lifting their perceptions, or they can dismiss them in favor of feeling their own way through the spiritual maze. Seeking a balance through both is always an alternative.

One way of initiating balance is to call upon the Ancestral Spirit. If you have a difficult relationship with a family member, try the following technique. Use the fingers of one hand to find the pulse in your carotid artery next to your windpipe. For our purposes this represents the area of the voice and therefore communication itself. Once you feel your pulse, match the beat with the other hand. Remember the rhythm of your heartbeat.

Think of someone who causes you disharmony or pain in any way. Place a picture of them on a table in front of you. If you do not have a picture, then you can simply write the person's name on a piece of paper. The next step is to tap your finger on the photo or the paper, then say the following words:

"Ancestors come to beating of our heart, to the flow of our blood, to the movement of our breath." Pause for a few moments, and then continue: *"I am sorry for this situation of disharmony, of ill feeling."* Pause again for a few moments. Continue with these words:

"I choose to forgive and to be forgiven for this discord inside me. It is how I see others from my place of assigning fault. Ancestors, I ask that you enter in and cleanse the blood that has become a sea of storm. I love and ask for love."

This is part of the process that I call closing the gate of day and opening the gate of night. It is a deliberate act to quell, and a deliberate act to invite reunion. One action moves another into play; it is like tipping one domino at the head of a row of them. One by one they all give way to the action of the preceding one.

Many gates open into the inner and outer mysteries. In ancient lore we find the Star Gates of the Pleiades. This constellation marks the time of May and of October (November

Eve). Attached to these times we find the mythos of the Seven Sisters of the Pleiades. In one mystical tradition they guide souls into the material world and then escort them into the next world. In the inner tradition this is the initiating of a process that begins in May and culminates at the end of October (literally November Eve).

In the mythos the Seven Sisters open the Gates of the Pleiades. The year of your birth is one such opening in its time, as is the year of your death. Just as birth may come early or late in the scheme of things, so too is it with death. The latter can come at pivotal moments and can bypass those moments as well.

One belief is that the Seven Sisters guide souls (those reincarnating) into new lives and then accompany them on their journey. This involves directing them to places of enlightenment and pivotal moments in each lifetime. We can think of this as one's "lucky stars" or guiding stars.

On another level, the Seven Sisters lead one to the Center of Life, to the personal axis mundi. Reportedly the Mayan and Egyptian pyramids were aligned with the Pleiades, and in this we can see these structures as a type of axis mundi. In the myths of some ancient cultures we find the Pleiades depicted as swans or a boat/ark in the night sky. In this we can see them as connecting heaven and earth.

The Mayans, like several American Indian tribes such as the Cherokee, believe their Ancestors came from the Pleiades. The Mayans point to the star we now know as Alcyone as their home star. The Mayan calendar (the Tzolk'in) was based upon the movement or cycles of the Pleiades. This intimate connection and focus on this constellation seems to suggest a basis for the concept of the "First Ancestors" or "Star-People" who were encountered in a previous chapter.

The Mayans performed human sacrifice during rites associated with the planet Venus, which has long been referred to as a "star" in several ancient cultures. It has been called both the evening and morning star. In an earlier chapter we noted that the Greek god Hersperus was associated with Venus and fathered the first Guardians of Immortality (the Hesperides). In Roman mythology Venus (called Lucifer by the Romans, and Phosphorus by the Greeks) was known as the Herald of the Sun. The name "Lucifer" means "Light Bearer" but has become distorted by Christian notions into the figure of Satan (the Devil) who appears in Christian biblical myths.

In the Cabalistic teachings of the Tree of Life, Venus is related to Tipareth (the world of the human soul). The sphere of Venus is also known as the Causal World, which is the realm of willpower). It is here that we find the monad, which is a trio of Spirit, Divine Soul, and Human Soul. In this we can see a similarity to the Three Selves that are the basis for the teachings in this book.

The "lower" part of the Human Soul, in Cabalistic thought, is bound up in fleshly desires, and is therefore contaminated by base vibrations. Where some religions regard this as the negative influence of Lucifer, most esoteric systems see Lucifer as the liberator. Lucifer, as the light-bearer, offers the rungs of a ladder upon which Human Consciousness can climb up from the things that deflect its vision of the Divine emanations. We must climb and reach the axis mundi, we must reach the summit from which communication between Above and Below burns as a sacred flame before us.

The idea of the flame brings us to such figures as the tarot's hermit who holds the star lantern. This is connected to the idea of the flames emanated by the First Ancestors, the star gods. The classic image of the hermit depicts him standing on a mountaintop. He holds a star enclosed in a lantern. His light shines from on high, a beacon that calls to true seekers. The star flame shines; it is the soul recognized by Human Consciousness as the guiding force.

In the Hidden Path divination deck we find the elder staff card. It depicts a person holding a staff and moving away down an old road. The Elder has left behind the previous world and has passed through the gate. He or she moves along a rustic path walking towards a new horizon. Rising up on the horizon is a starry sky with a full moon shining down. In this imagery we can see the walk of one who has attained enlightenment. The Elder passes in the Gates of Evening, leaving behind that which no longer serves. The staff represents the World Tree, the ladder upon which the Elder will climb up into stars. In this the soul returns to the stars, Human Consciousness rises to the Lunar Realm of the Dead, and the body returns to elements beneath.

The Gates of Evening are the constellations above us. Many mythical beings and heroes have been placed in the night sky. The Ancestral myths and legends are written in the stars. In each life we connect with our astrological sign. The myth and attributes of our sun sign (the sun being a star) resonate in the blended Three Selves. What we find in the earthly understanding of our stellar story leads us to the inner realization of our star-self. We need but enter through the Gates of Evening.

CHAPTER 9

The Rites of Connection

Presented in this chapter are various rites and practices you can use in the veneration of your Ancestors. I have integrated many old customs, observances, and practices in these rites while at the same time keeping them pertinent to contemporary times. In this way the connections contained in these rites are ever ancient and ever new. I believe this will serve both the traditionalist and the eclectic tastes.

The majority of these rituals are connected to "hearth and home" application, but I have also included other rites that can be performed outdoors. There is, in particular, a ritual for use in a cemetery. Additionally you will find rites for redeeming the Ancestors and making peace with them and the Dead. Along with them is a ritual for asking release from wrongs you (or others) have done to people who are still alive. This can help diminish the "karmic" energy carried from this lifetime into the next. It is, in effect, a preemptive action.

I suggest compiling some standard items to incorporate in your Ancestral ritual practice. Trust your intuition in regards to using each item for a specific purpose or rite. Here is a general list for review:

- White birch bark
- White candle
- Black candle
- Red candle

- Human skull replica
- Offering bowl and cup
- Incense
- Silver bell
- Ancestral link (photo, cultural image, or heirloom)

The Threshold Ritual

In ancient thought, the threshold of a doorway was a liminal or in-between place. It was magical because it was neither inside nor outside, and in such places, spirits were believed to lurk and hide. To step directly on the threshold was believed to bring misfortune or to evoke unknown changes or events. One belief is that this is the reason why brides were carried over the threshold; it was intended to keep the couple from entering their new home with threshold spirits attached to them.

In keeping with ancient thought, the following simple ritual can be used to bless the threshold. This will ensure that only positive entities can dwell on the threshold. Perform this ritual before entering a new home. It can also be used to set things right at the threshold of a home that is already occupied. For this ritual you will need two green candles, a bowl with clean water, a dry cloth, a teaspoon of salt, a handful of mint leaves, and a small bell to ring with your hand. Once you have all of this ready you can perform the rite as follows:

1. Place a green candle inside the doorway, light it, and say: *"Here burns the light of the Evergreen Spirit of Nature."* Next trace an "X" with your index finger in front of the candle, and say: *"Here stands the Green Guardian; no spirit of ill intent may enter across this threshold."*

2. Dip your thumb, index finger, and middle finger (together) into the bowl of water. Then use them to sprinkle the threshold with some water, moving from left to right. As you do this, say: *"Water, purifier and dissolver, cleanse and remove from this threshold all that is negative, unbalanced, destructive, and disharmonious."* Repeat this three times.

3. Take the cloth, and moving from the inside of the door to the outside, wipe the threshold, saying: *"I remove from this threshold all that is negative, unbalanced, destructive, and disharmonious."* Set the cloth aside when you are finished.

4. Hold the bell over the threshold and ring it three times, saying before each ring: *"I dispel from the air here, all which is negative, unbalanced, destructive, and disharmonious."*

5. From left to right, sprinkle or scatter the mint leaves across the threshold, while saying: *"All is welcome here that is positive, balanced, constructive, and harmonious."*

6. Set the other green candle on the outside of the threshold and light it, saying: "Here burns the Evergreen Spirit, that which prevails against all decline, diminishment, and ending." Trace an equilateral cross in front of the candle, and say: *"Here stands the Evergreen Guardian Spirit; no spirit may approach or pass by that is negative, unbalanced, destructive, or disharmonious."*

7. Take the salt and sprinkle it along the outer edge of the threshold, moving form left to right, and say: *"Strict charge and watch I set, that to this place no evil thing may approach nor enter in."*

Complete the rite by sitting with candles for a couple of minutes as they continue to burn. When you are ready to finish, blow out the inside candle first and then the outside one. Remove all the items, leaving the salt and mint leaves in place at least overnight. This concludes the ritual.

The Hearth Ritual

For our Ancestors, the hearth or fireplace was always the setting for preparing meals and gathering the family together. This is a strong connection that has endured the ages. The following ritual is designed to create a sacred center within the home that is reminiscent of the spirit of our Ancestors. It is a place where you can join the past with the present through the portal of the fireplace. If you do not have a fireplace you can use a model fashioned like one (some are made to fit a votive or tea light candle).

To perform this ritual you will need two candles: one white and one red. You will also need an evergreen wreath, a bowl of fresh water, a handful of grain of some type, a bell, a platter, and a glass of red wine. Once these items are ready, proceed as follows:

1. Set the wreath inside the opening of the hearth (or fireplace). In the center of the wreath place a white candle.
2. Put the bowl of water in front of the opening to the hearth/fireplace. The bowl is in-between you and the wreath.
3. Light the white candle in the wreath, and say: *"White is the bone memory. I give the welcome of light for those who came before."*
4. Dip your fingers into the bowl of water and sprinkle the wreath, saying: *"Life sustainer to life retainer:*

Let this place be a pure pool to quench all thirst and a circle of life to join all generations."

5. Remove the bowl of water and set the platter there with grain on it. Next to the platter set the glass of red wine. Ring the bell over these items, and then say: *"Ancestors I call to you to come to this place and partake of these offerings."* (Sit quietly with this for a few moments.)

6. Place the red candle in front of the offerings, light it, and say: *"Blood to blood I call my own, blood to blood be all at home."*

Close the ritual by talking with your Ancestors. Let it be known that you want them to be present in your life, and that our hearth/fireplace is a symbol of gathered family, past and present. When you feel it is time to finish, then put all the items away.

Because the red candle represents the family blood, you may want to light a red candle by the hearth/fireplace on family occasions.

Ancestral Shrine

The setting of an Ancestral Shrine is very simple. The purpose of the shrine is to honor people you loved and thought highly of and who impacted your life in positive ways. The advantage of a shrine versus an altar is its small size and general appearance (so as not to have too many questions asked by visitors to your home).

This type of shrine is ideal in small spaces. In essence it can be a shelf, the top of an end table or nightstand, a fireplace mantle, and so on. On the shrine you will place framed photos of departed loved ones, family, and friends. You may also want to lay a nice cloth over the surface area, and then arrange the picture frames as you wish. The last items are a vase for flowers and a candleholder with white candle. You can add more items if you like, but this is the basic setup.

Ideally you will want to acknowledge and honor family occasions on your shrine. For example you can place flowers and light a candle for birthdays, anniversaries, weddings, funerals, and special family events such as graduations and various achievements. In this way your Ancestors are invited in to be part of the celebration.

To set up the Ancestral Shrine requires little more than a blessing ceremony. Once you select an area for the shrine then plan your arrangement of items. Try to have all photos visible with none blocking any of the others. Depending upon how many photo frames you are using, you can set some on a stand to lift them higher so as not to be blocked. Place the larger frames in the back and the smaller ones in front to be easily seen.

A nice way to arrange the shrine is to have the flower vase and the candleholder flanking the photos (one off to each side). The traditional choice of a color for a candle is white, which represents the bone memory. However you can also certainly use other colored candles. For example, add candles in accord with the seasons or colors that were favored by those who have passed into the next world. Do the same with flowers on your shrine.

One final touch is to offer special food or drink to remember and honor a particular departed loved one on his or her former birthday. For example, when my father passed away I placed his favorite candy in a bowl in front of his picture. He was very fond of licorice, and so I gave him assorted pieces in a bowl each day for awhile. One teaching is that the newly dead remain in the vicinity for seven days following their death, and this is the period of daily offerings I subscribe to in my practices.

Now that you have a good idea of the shrine's layout, here is the blessing to complete it and make it active. To begin, light a stick of incense that you favor. Hold it over the shrine and move it in a downward spiral motion (symbolizing the shrine as a place to enter and abide). Do this three times as you say the blessing: "I connect with what I hold to be Divinity, and in that presence I pass blessings of Light into this shrine. Ancestors and loved ones now departed from me in form, you are welcome here, and the light is always on to guide your return."

To Call the Ancestors

This ritual is designed to connect you with your Ancestors in shared consciousness. While the Ancestors are never truly separated from us, we are not always holding them in our awareness. This ritual will place you in intentional space with them, mind, body, and soul. For this rite you will need a black candle, a red candle, and a white candle. You will also need an offering of food and drink and a bell. Ideally you should use something that has a cultural connection to your Ancestors. When everything is assembled, you can move to performing the ritual.

1. Begin by lighting the three candles: one black, one red, and one white. Once all the candles have flames, ring the bell over each one, and then say: *"Here burn the Three Great Mysteries: Where did I come from, why am I here, and what happens after this life?"*

2. Place the food and drink between you and the candles.
3. Ring the bell three times, each time saying the following words:
   "Hear me Ancestors,
   I call upon the wind into your realm.
   Come to our shared breath
   Come to our shared blood
   Come to our shared bone."
4. Place fingertips somewhere on your body where you can feel your pulse beat. Feel it for a few moments, and then say the following words: *"Ancestors, together we hear the beating of the drum across time. It is the drumming up of the blood. Once it flowed in you, and is now passed to me. I carry the drum, I am its beating heart."*
5. Place the palms of both hands facedown over and above the food and drink offerings, and say: *"Ancestors, I have set this food and drink in your honor. I invite you to the meal; share with me now and let us renew our family bonds."* (Eat and drink a small portion, leaving the bulk of it for the Ancestors.)
6. Once the meal has ended, sit comfortably and perform the following. Lightly press your fingertips and thumbs together, meeting their counterparts. While keeping them together, bend them so that your hands form a sphere between them. If done correctly your hands will look as though they are holding an imaginary ball. In doing this you are establishing the Ancestral Eye.

7. Slowly bring the *eye* up to your forehead, close your eyes, and say: *"Ancestor, Spirit-Rider, look now into the World of Light. See me, see my walk, and lend me your vision that my path is guided in all right ways."*

8. Spend a few minutes in meditation and communication with the Ancestral Spirit. Be receptive, listen, and do not hold expectations.

9. When you feel ready to conclude, press the Ancestral Eye against the center of your forehead, and say: *"Ancestor, I take in and receive your vision and your guidance."*

10. Conclude now with the release. Ring the bell three times over the black, red, and white candles, and then say: *"Ancestors, I thank you for your presence. And as you return now back into your realm, may there always be peace between us. May you always look with favor upon me."*

11. Extinguish the candles and put everything away. The ritual is concluded.

Prayer to the Ancestors

"Ancestors, we are of the one bone,
We are of the one blood,
We are of the one spirit.
Come, Spirit-Rider,
and together we will see each other's world.
Come, Sprit-Rider, and fetch me,
take me to the places of my Ancestors.
Come, Spirit-Rider,
come and place me in the visions that open my mind.

Fetch me to starry realms
and return me illuminated with their Light."

Ancestral Altar

The veneration of our Ancestors is a very ancient practice that appears widespread in many different lands. Your Ancestors can offer guidance and protection, and they can bestow their wisdom to you in the form of inner teachings.

The Ancestral altar is a formal setup as compared to the shrine. Because it is an altar it calls for a deeper practice than does the general shrine. The Ancestral altar bears the symbols of life and death. It is used to call upon both the Ancestors and the spirits of the Dead.

The altar layout is as follows. Drape the altar space with either a black or white cloth. Black represents the Otherworld, and white represents the bone memory of all who came before us. Near the back and center area of the altar place a replica of a human skull. In front of it place two replicas of the thigh bones (crossed to form an X shape) The skull represents your Ancestral lineage, and the crossbones represent the gateway (opened or closed). If you cannot find replicas of thigh bones to use, you can substitute twigs (painted white).

On top of the skull place a red candle, this will symbolize the life's blood that flows through the generations to your own body. It is a link to the concept of the Living River of Blood. In front of the skull and crossbones place a small platter and a wineglass. Near the front of the altar, off to the left side, set a bowl of fresh water. You will renew the water each time you activate the altar. On the right side of the altar (directly across from the bowl) place a stone of your choosing. Between the two items set a twig (no longer than a foot).

Ideally the twig should be of birch, although willow, yew, or cypress will do nicely as well.

In addition to the aforementioned here is a list of other items for a formal Ancestral altar:

- Two candleholders
- Two candles, one white and one red
- One pack of spelt grain (one of the oldest traditional offerings)
- Anointing oil (your choice)
- Two cords: red and white to symbolize the living bloodline (red) and the ancient memory (white)

When all the items are assembled, you can begin the ritual.

1. On each side of the skull set a candleholder. The one on the right holds the red candle and the one on the left holds the white candle. Take the red cord and place one end touching the candleholder on the right and extend the other end towards you (making a line from the candle to you). Do the same with the candleholder on the left, using the white cord extended from that candleholder.

2. Light all the candles. Then touch the water and the stone with the twig lying between them. As you do, say these words: *"Water, you dissolve all things; part now the veil between the Otherworld and the Mortal Realm. Stone, you give form and hold all things in place; be now a temporary anchor for beings of light entering the material world."*

3. Anoint your wrist pulse areas with the oil. Call to your Ancestors: *"Hear me my Ancestors, I call*

to you from blood and bone. I call to you from the memory within, the memory you have passed from the bodies you once wore. You are in me and I am in you." (Now separate the crossbones to create an open area to and from the skull. In this configuration the tips of each crossbone will point towards you.)

4. Make an offering of grain on the platter, and fill the glass with wine. Then, touch the ends of the cords closest to you with your fingertips (resting your hands on the surface of the altar). Speak these words: *"Hear me, my Ancestors, you who have come before me. I am the bearer of our bloodline. I am the current steward of the Living River of Blood. I am the present, reaching into the past, and carrying us all into the future."* (Pause for a few moments in honor of the Ancestors partaking of the offerings.) Following this phase you can ask for guidance, oracle vision, wisdom, protection, or whatever feels needed. Ask to be taught and contacted in your dreams. Later you will discover other means and times for contact. But for now the dream state is advisable. When you are done, it is time to bid farewell to your Ancestors until next time.

5. Touching the cord tips with your fingers, say these words: *"Ancestors, I thank you for your presence and blessings here upon your altar. As you now depart to your lovely realms, may there always be peace between us, may you always look with favor upon me."* (Place the stone in the bowl of water, wash it, and say: *"I release all from this stone."*)

6. Place the crossbones back into the X position (thereby closing the gate).
7. Pick up the white and red cords and coil them into a sphere shape. Set them off to each side of the skull.
8. Blow out the candles. Leave the offerings overnight, and then bury them the next day (or toss them in an open field or garden). The rite is concluded.

Ritual for Healing the Ancestors

This ritual is designed to introduce healing and redemptive energy in the Ancestral current. Through this the Ancestors can be relieved of negative imprints in their energy that cause them disharmony of the spirit. The energy we send them accomplishes our will under the "authority" we possess as the living keepers of the bloodline, the stewards of the Living River of Blood.

Perform this ritual after activating your Ancestral altar (as detailed in this chapter). Once that is performed, then use a different work area to present this ritual. Here you will need a clear crystal, an iris flower, a bowl of fresh water (with mint and lemon juice added), a red candle with holder, a replica of the human skull, a bell, and a stick of Dragon's Blood incense. Additionally you will need a sharp lance for piercing a finger, and a pouch for the crystal. When you have all these items assembled, you can begin the ritual.

1. Place the skull as the centerpiece of your work area. In front of it set the red candle. Place the bowl of water to the right of the skull and the incense to the left along with the bell. In front of the red candle set the crystal and the flower.
2. Light the red candle and the Dragon's blood incense.

3. Pick up the incense stick and move your hand over the skull in a spiraling fashion (clockwise). As you do this, say the following words: *"Hear me, my Ancestors, I call to you from blood and bone. I call to you from the memory within, the memory you have passed from the bodies you once wore. You are in me and I am in you. Hear me, Ancestors, I call upon the wind into your realm. Come to our shared breath. Come to our shared blood. Come to our shared bone."* (Now ring the bell three times.)

4. Take the lance and pierce one your fingers. Squeeze out three drops of blood into the bowl of water. Tend to your wound, and then proceed by holding the palms of both hands facedown over the water. Then, say these words: *"I declare my authority as the living keeper of the River of Blood. I declare my authority as the reigning steward of my blood lineage."*

5. In your right hand carry the smoking incense stick to each of the Four Directions: East, South, West, and North. In your left hand carry the bowl of water. At each quarter, say these words:

   East: *"Elemental Spirits of Air, transmit the wounds of my Ancestors into the healing water that dissolves away all fault."*

   South: *"Elemental Spirits of Fire, transform the wounds of my Ancestors within the healing water that dissolves away all fault."*

   West: *"Elemental Spirits of Water, move the wounds of my Ancestors into the healing water that dissolves away all fault."*

North: *"Elemental Spirits of Earth, condense the wounds of my Ancestors into the healing water that dissolves away all fault."*

6. Return the incense and the bowl of water to the work area.

7. Place the palms of both hands downward over the bowl of water. Next, looking at the skull, say these words: *"Ancestors, behold the faults herein that are your wounds; self-inflicted or inflicted by others. Behold what binds you from liberation."*

8. Pick up the crystal in your right hand, and say: *"Here is the gem of liberation; here is the releaser of all that keeps you bound."*

9. Drop the crystal into the water, and then hold your palms over the bowl again, saying: *"Ancestors hear me, by my place as Steward of our Lineage, by my place as Living Keeper of the River of Blood, by the power of my breath and bone and blood do I draw into this crystal all that binds your spirit to fault."*

10. Remove the crystal and put it directly in the pouch.

11. Dip your fingers in the water and lift them up so that water runs back into the bowl. Do this several times. Then carry the bowl to the Four Directions, and at each one stir the water again as before, and say:

    East: *"Elemental Spirits of Air, transmit your refreshing breath of life into this water."*

    South: *"Elemental Spirits of Fire, send transforming flames to purity this water."*

    West: *"Elemental Spirits of Water, move freshness into this liquid to renew its purity."*

    North: *"Elemental Spirits of Earth, retain the water anew in this clean vessel."*

12. Return the bowl to the work area, setting it in front of the skull. Then, say: *"The water is clean and renewed. It is free of all contagion."*

13. Pick up the skull, hold it over the water, and then with a free hand wash the skull completely, saying: *"Ancestors be washed clean and be renewed. All fault is gone, all blame is rinsed, all debt is forgiven. I am the steward of our lineage, and I say it is so."*

14. End the rite by cleaning up the area and removing the items and debris. The crystal should be set outside in the noonday sun for an hour. After this it should be buried away from the home.

Ritual for Soul Mending

In the views of very old systems, such as Huna, we find the belief in an attachment to ill treatment. The teaching is that an etheric cord connects the wrong-doer to the injured party. As long as the person continues to hold on to that cord, an active connection remains in place. Among the Kahuna this is defined as "fault" or what they call "hala." The energy of hala establishes a "debt" between the two people linked by the cord. This causes an inner sorrow for the injured party holding the cord, and it causes disharmony for the wrong-doer on the other end (even though the latter may not consciously be aware of its effects).

The energy held as *fault* can travel from generation to generation and often results in feuds of one time or another. It can be inherited by a family or an organization of people. In cases where the fault has been egregious, the attachment can even bind itself to a nation. One example is the atrocities we see take place during times of war. These do not simply go away when the war ends. To cure the contagion of fault, its connective cord energy must be "untied" and the fault must be released. This will allow healing to begin to take place.

This ritual is designed to release negative connections to people who wronged you or who you wronged in this lifetime. In cases where you have lost touch with such a person, or it is best not to have any relationship with them, this is the ideal ritual. For the rite you will need a bowl of water, some incense to burn, and a small thin, dry twig that is easy to break with your hands. When all is in place, begin as follows:

1. Sit quietly in a comfortable spot and have the bowl of water and the incense in front of you. Hold the twig in your dominant hand. Spend a few moments thinking about the misdeeds that connect you to the other person.

2. Light the incense, and then say these words: *"It is my will and desire to be released from what holds my thoughts and feelings connected to (name person) and therefore keeps the past here in the present."*

3. Say the person's name, and then blow on the incense so that your words are carried out upon your breath.

4. Hold the twig in the incense smoke, and say: *"Soul of [person's name], hear my voice, soul to soul. I seek release from fault, fault is in the past. It is a shadow of what once was; it has no place between us for it is nothing done here in the present. It is a specter that I release now into light, and it vanishes."* Blow your breath into the incense smoke.

5. Set the twig aside, and dip the fingertips of both hands into the bowl of water. Then lift them and

allow the water to drip back into the bowl. Do this three times, each time, saying the following: *"I cleanse the space that held fault, it holds it no more."*

6. With the fingers of one hand slowly stir the incense counterclockwise, saying these words as you do so: *"For what fault was yours, I release you from it. There is no need or desire for recompense due or owed. For what fault was mine, I release my attachment to it; soul to soul let there be forgiveness and release."*

7. Hold the twig in the incense smoke with one hand on each end, and say these words: *"Let all hurt be broken away, all anger be severed, and all breach of faith be set asunder in mind, body, and spirit."* Forcefully snap the twig in half. Then throw it outdoors, focusing your feelings on the act of throwing it and all it represents away. Pour the bowl of water on the earth, away from your property line. Let the incense burn out.

8. Take a bath or shower to cleanse yourself. As the water drains away, so too does any attachment to the past.

Ritual for Harmony of the Inner Selves

This ritual is designed to harmonize your three inner selves so that communication is not blocked or distorted. It is a "self-blessing" of sorts but also an alignment. You should pick a day each month as a routine for performing this ritual. You should also perform this ritual whenever you feel disturbed, upset, sad, or discouraged.

For this rite you will need four candles: black, red, white, and green. The red candle will represent the Elemental Body that carries the life blood. The black candle represents

Human Consciousness because black is symbolic of full potentiality and procreation. The white candle represents the soul as white is the color of what endures. The green candle represents peace and harmony. In addition to the candles you will also need a bowl of fresh water, some oil for anointing your body, and a small portion of the herbs thyme and Dittany of Crete. In addition choose a flower of your liking; it will be used to sprinkle the water. When all is assembled proceed as follows:

1. Remove all clothing. In this way all the selves are equal.

2. Set three of the candles in a line side by side from your left to your right. The order is red, black, and white. Sprinkle the mixture of herbs around their base (these herbs are associated with communication and blessings).

3. Dip the flower into the water and sprinkle it on your genitals, three times, saying: *"With this water that dissolves all things, I wash away all that blocks the energy and the consciousness of my Elemental Body. I release all that prevents clear and unobstructed communication between my Three Selves."* (Light the red candle and pause for a moment, seeing it as glowing spirit of the Elemental Body.)

4. Dip the flower back in the water and sprinkle it on your forehead, three times, saying: *"With this water that dissolves all things, I wash away all that blocks the energy of my Human Consciousness. I release all that prevents clear and unobstructed communication between my Three Selves."* (Light the

black candle and pause for a moment, seeing it as glowing spirit of Human Consciousness.)

5. Dip the flower in the water again and sprinkle it on the area of your solar plexus three times, saying: *"With this water that dissolves all things, I wash away all that blocks the energy and the consciousness of my Soul Body. I release all that prevents clear and unobstructed communication between my inner selves."* (Light the white candle and pause for a moment, seeing it as glowing spirit of the Soul Body.)

6. Now you will begin the process of spiraling energy into each center (each Self). This is done with the clockwise motion of your dominant hand. Beginning with the genital area, create the spiral in a slow-moving fashion, and say: *"Elemental Body, we, the Human Consciousness and Soul Body, find no fault in you, hold no fault to you. We send love and acceptance into your being. With you we are whole. Let communication freely flow between us."*

7. Begin to spiral in the area of your forehead, and say: *"Human Consciousness, we, the Elemental Body and Soul Body, find no fault in you, hold no fault to you. We send love and acceptance into your being. With you we are whole. Let communication freely flow between us."*

8. Begin to spiral over the solar plexus area, and say: *"Soul Body, we, the Elemental Body and Human Consciousness, find no fault in you, hold no fault to you. We send love and acceptance into your being. With you we are whole. Let communication freely flow between us."*

9. Look upon the three burning candles that represent the Three Selves. Spend a few moments watching their flames. Are they equal? Is one moving different from another? If so, address the flames that are different by saying: *"No fault exists, no fault can be found, all is blessed."* (At this phase no longer concern yourself about the flames.)

10. Pause again for a moment while looking at the three lighted candles. See them as the spirits of all showing their flame. Then take the green candle, anoint it with the oil, and beginning from the left, slowly pass its wick through all three flames (making sure it is lighted by the first candle). This symbolizes the joining of all three into one flame, the light of flowing communication. As you pass the green candle, say: *"I join the free flowing flames of the Three Selves into one voice of light."* (Anoint yourself with the oil: genital area, forehead, and solar plexus.)

11. Next you will extinguish the red, black, and white candles in the following manner. Set the lighted green candle down and a couple of feet away from you. Stand, and in order of red, black, and white, blow each one out in the direction of the green candle (as though the flame passes into the green candle as opposed to being extinguished). Keep that imagery in mind. As you blow out each candle, say: *"I pass the symbol of your harmony into the one flame."*

12. When all three candles are extinguished, put them aside and pick up the lighted green candle. Focus on its flame, and say: *"In you the Three Selves are one flame in peace, harmony, and flowing communication."*

13. Let the candle sit for a few moments as you bask in the feeling. When you are ready to finish the rite, blow it out after saying: *"Breath of the Ancestors, breathe in what here goes out."*

14. At later times should you feel low, you can light the green candle as a way to renew and refresh the inner connection of peace, harmony, and the self-connection. Simply breathe out across the candle, and then light it, saying: *"Breath of the Ancestors, breathe out what herein goes."*

You can repeat the entire rite at a future time as you feel it is needed.

Ritual for Infant or Child Blessing

This is a ritual for welcoming a new life. It is based upon a tradition that I practice but can be modified for use in any way that suits your views. Read this blessing rite over beforehand to see what is needed and what you may want to change.

The Ceremony

1. Mark a circle on the ground/floor with flowers or leaves (the rose plant is ideal). The circle should be large enough to fit all attendees.

2. The child is blessed with anointing of rose scented oil on the soles of feet and forehead. You may want to test ahead to make sure there are no allergy problems to deal with. It is unlikely, but better to be safe than sorry, as the saying goes. Words of blessing when anointing: *"May the Divine look upon you always with great favor, and may your days be filled with all that is good in life. In the light*

of Divine Emanation, may it be so." (Anyone in attendance repeats: *"May it be so."*)

3. Parents: Place hands on the infant/child, and say: *"You have entered into this world in our care and stewardship. We accept this role and will faithfully keep to your well-being."*

4. The child is then presented to the Four Quarters, and each is addressed.

    East: *"Powers of the East, we ask that you bestow upon this little one your gifts of lofty thoughts, good mindfulness, and gainful enlightenment."*

    South: *"Powers of the South, we ask that you bestow upon this little one your gifts of empowerment, benevolent passion, and constructive transformative vision."*

    West: *"Powers of the West, we ask that you bestow upon this little one your gifts of forward movement, proper adaptation, and successful direction."*

    North: *"Powers of the North, we ask that you bestow upon this little one your gifts of balanced strength, rightful stability, and conquering endurance."*

5. After presenting to the Four Quarters, the infant/child is brought to a comfortable place. A red rose is then held above her or him, and these words are spoken: *"Here beneath the sacred rose that joins all in the power of love may its spirit open the memory of the earth to you that your journey through this life be enriched by all that has come before you."* (Tap feet and hands with rose three times.)

*6. Members of the family and friends may now come forward and offer tokens to the infant/child which symbolize their wishes (for the child as she or he grows). Upon presentation, the person will say the child's name, and then say: *"I wish for you (name of virtue or wish, etc.)."* These items should be kept for the child and later placed in a special pouch or bag to be stored in the child's room.

Ceremony is concluded. Close the circle and proceed with social occasion.

* Some examples of tokens:

- A red rose: love, honor, beauty, and sacredness
- A shell: abundance and fullness in life
- A raven's feather: wisdom, cunning, and a sense of humor
- A flower: spiritual gifts of healing and cleansing
- A stone: strength and fortitude; strong in nature
- A hawk's feather: hunting skills and keen senses
- A stag horn: virility and strong ties to Clan; personal power
- A coin: prosperity
- A pinch of mint leaves: health and well-being
- A rabbit's foot: good luck

Funeral Rite

This is a ritual for releasing the departed and blessing him or her for the journey of the Afterlife. It is based upon a tradition that I practice but can be modified for use in any way that suits your views. Read the following over beforehand to see what is needed and what you may want to change.

In preparation, the body should be anointed with pennyroyal oil shortly after death (pennyroyal emanates a high spiritual vibration). Ideally the body should be cremated along with some cedar, sandalwood, and juniper wood (old symbols of mystical transformation). This rite is designed with the theme of cremation, and that the ashes are present during the funeral.

A symbol of a white birch tree is placed in the setting of the funeral. Red and white roses are set on an altar. A bowl half-filled with water, a twig, and a small stone are also set on the altar. Additionally a "spirit candle" representing the departed is set on the altar (ideally the favorite color of the departed person). With the candle, set some incense that will be burned later in the rite, and place a ritual bell for tolling. A birch wand or staff is set on, or next to, the altar. A photo of the departed can be placed for viewing next to the ash urn.

The Ceremony

1. At the site of the funeral, the facilitator addresses those assembled: *"We have come to the time now when (name of person) must begin the sacred journey to the Afterlife."* (Spirit candle is now lighted.) *"(Name of person), you know now the Mystery, which is forgotten while in this life, and you have therefore entered into the greatest of all rites of passage."*

   The facilitator addresses the attendees: *"Let us not bind our friend/loved one to this material world with our longing for her/him to be with us still. Let us not burden her/his spirit too long with our sorrow. Let us release her/him with love, even as a parent must free a child who has grown to adulthood. Blessed be (name of person), we wish you love and light to be with you on your journey, and happiness within the beautiful realm into which you pass. Blessed be (all repeat)."*

2. Ritual bell tolls thrice. The facilitator then introduces anyone who wishes to speak about the departed. Memories may be shared, deeds retold, and so on.

3. Ritual bell tolls again three times. Each person attending the funeral may come forward now before the vessel containing the ashes and personally bid their friend farewell. Singing or chanting may begin at this time while people pay their respects in private.

The Releasing:

4. The facilitator addresses the attendees: *"We come now to the time of releasing (name of person) from the world of mortalkind so that she/he may begin the journey to the Afterlife in liberation."*

5. The facilitator holds hands (palm down) over the bowl, and says: *"Here is the vessel of transformation, the magical vessel that is the portal between the worlds."*

6. The facilitator (at the altar) holds up the stone over the bowl of water, and says: *"This is form, this is that which holds the spirit to the world of matter."*

7. The facilitator places right hand (palm down) over the water, and says: *"This is that which dissolves all forms."*

8. The facilitator speaks the name of the departed, lowers the stone into the bowl of water, and says: *"Be washed clean of the form that bound you to the material world. Dissolved away is all that held you to material form."*

9. The facilitator holds the twig over the water, and says: *"Here is that which ever renews, here is the promise of the evergreen spirit that is never extinguished."* The twig is then lowered into the water and left there.

10. Facilitator: *"What is drawn into the world of matter also withdraws from the world of matter. Such is the cycle; such is the journey through the Wheel of the Year. As it is above, so is it below."* Facilitator takes the birch wand or staff in hand, addresses the departed by name, and then says: *"You have come to this journey's end. This world of mortalkind is but a dream now from which you shall soon awaken. All who came before you, call now from across the distant stars. The Isle of the Moon glistens like a jewel upon the waters of the Otherworld. It is time now to take your leave and to journey to your restful place. The Forest breathes you in, and the branches of the White Tree show you the way to the realm beyond. In the breath of the Greenwood you are lovingly held. And through the breath of the Greenwood you shall be breathed back into life once again."*

11. The facilitator places the lighted "spirit candle" in front of the burning incense, and a white rose behind the incense, then speaks the name of the departed, and says: *"You came to us descended from the stars, fated by the sun, envisioned by the moon, given form by the land. And you walked your days rooted in the memories held by the earth. Reach upward and return now to your place among the stars."* The candle flame is then blown out into the rising incense

smoke, symbolizing the release from this world into the next. The birch is then placed in the incense smoke, and moved to mark an X in the smoke, symbolizing the closing of the material gateway.

12. In conclusion the funeral prayer is recited: *"We release now our Brother/Sister who has crossed over and begun the sacred journey to the realm beyond. We wish her/him well on the journey, sending the emanations of our love and our friendship. We know that the sorrow that we feel is of our own making. Truly there has been no lasting loss among us, for we shall meet each other again in a future life to come. And we shall remember, and know each other, and love again. We shall speak her/his name at times of gathering so as to honor the memory of what we all shared together in the world of formation. May the Divine receive the soul of (name of person) into its care and may our Brother/Sister be given comfort and be prepared to be born anew. May the realm of beyond provide all that she/he needs and desires, and may she/he find peace and pleasure, and reunion with those who have gone before. Farewell dear brother/sister, farewell dear friend. Our love and blessings go with you."* The white rose is presented to the next of kin. The ashes are then scattered (or buried) and everyone may toss flowers or other tokens as the remains are received by the earth. The rite is completed.

Appendix I

Inner Mysteries of the Hearth

The hearth featured prominently in the lives of our Ancestors. On one level it served as the place to prepare and serve meals, and to warm the family as it gathered before the hearthside. There is, however, another element connected to the hearth that is of a mystical nature. It is here that we meet fire and its spirit.

Fire is among the most ancient symbols or representations of Divinity. One example appears in the ancient sect known as the vestal virgins who tended the sacred fire of the goddess Vesta. Her Greek counterpart is the goddess Hestia. In Greek culture Hestia was never depicted in art but images of Vesta are plentiful in ancient Mediterranean civilization. This may be connected to the theme as fire being the untamed or non-domesticated essence of the Divine.

Fire was a mysterious element in ancient times. Unlike elements of Earth, Air, and Water, Fire was not readily available in Nature. Our most distant Ancestors encountered fire when it fell from the sky in the form or lightning or issued from the earth as molten lava. Its relative rarity made the "fire keepers" or "fire tenders" key tribal members. In time our Ancestors discovered methods of producing fire through the use of flints, friction, and the application of a glass lens.

Over the course of time our Ancestors brought fire into the home. The hearth contained and kept it available each day throughout the year. Its spiritual or magical nature survived in such customs as the Need Fire of ancient Northern European culture. In times of disease or of infertility (of crops and animals) a special fire was lighted to restore the land and its inhabitants. All the hearth fires in the village were first extinguished before the Need Fire was ignited. The Need Fire was created upon a high hill. Once it was lighted, its fire was passed to a large stack of chopped wood to create a bonfire. It could be seen by all below in the village.

From among the fire tenders a person was chosen to light a torch. Holding the torch, he then ran down the hill into the village and lit a new hearth fire in each home. In this way the new and vitalized spirit entered into the home of the villagers. The hearth fire belonged to the family into whose care it was entrusted. It was a sacred presence.

In the traditional composition of the hearth we can see several things that connect it with Ancestral veneration. Its mantle is the ancient fallen tree that once served as a primitive altar. The stones and the opening into the hearth represent the ancient grotto, which was among the earliest places of veneration by our Ancestors. This is the cave, the entryway into the Otherworld and birth canal back into the realm of mortalkind. Within the hearth the Divine presence dwelled. It was contained and yet untamed.

Long ago women were the keepers of the flame, the guardians of the sacred fire. In their hands they held the tools of calling, nurturing, and strengthening. Such has it been since ancient times when fire burned in the sacred grotto and in the groves of the Goddess. For this was her spirit and her Divine presence.

Fire is the great transformer, and the creator of the mystic's tools. Fire transforms the clay into the sacred pentacle of magic. It forges the chalice and the blade. Fire dwells as the

Divine flame within the wand. For the ancients believed that fire dwelled within wood waiting to be coaxed out.

In the ancient groves of the Goddess bundles of tree branches were gathered for torches. When a new grove was established, a bundle of branches was carried to the new site. Here the fire was drawn from the wood in a belief that the Divine essence of the Goddess was thereby evoked. Thus was the spirit of the Goddess passed from grove to grove.

Born of the fire of the Goddess, the tools connect with the Divine spark that is at the center of all things. Here is where the mystic touches the Otherworld and unites the material and the spiritual. The msytic's tools are the vehicles through which occult forces are drawn and channeled. One such tool is the cauldron set before the hearth. The cauldron symbolizes the womb and the womb-gate of the Goddess. All is born from her and to her all things return.

Some folklorists refer to the ancient belief that the hearth is the gateway to the Ancestral Realm. The fire in the hearth safeguarded against spirits of ill intent and allowed departed souls of the family line to return for visits. In Italy, one such spirit is called Befana. She enters the home through the chimney and represents the Ancestral Spirit that keeps the connection alive between the past and present generations. Woven socks, symbols of the Fate Weavers, were once hung on the chimney with offerings in them of fruit and nuts. This was intended to appease the Fates and bring favor to the living generation.

The Hearthside Bonds

Anthropologist Alessandro Falassi writes, in his book *Folklore by the Fireside,* of a centuries-old hearthside tradition. Here he describes the old "world by the fireplace" in peasant culture. Falassi tells us of the custom known as the *Veglia* (pronounced vay-yah). The earliest references to the Veglia in literature date from the 15th century, although almost certainly this was a much older practice.

The word essentially means to "keep watch" or remain vigilant, and is similar to the Latin word *vigilia*, meaning to stay awake during the usual hours of sleep. The Veglia has always been a social occasion in which social rules and values are discussed and transmitted in rural Tuscany; for centuries, folklore has provided the means and messages of such crucial communicative events.

Falassi describes the scene in which Italian peasants once returned from the fields at sunset and gathered before the fireplace. Here they began the night by telling fairytales to the youngest children. These contained various messages and morals intended to merge the child into the Tuscan community as she or he grew up. Next in order of age the children were told stories of their family members and Ancestors. This established a sense of who they were and who they had been. Lastly they spoke of their religious beliefs and customs in order to preserve their traditions. It is because of traditions like the Veglia that so much of the Old Ways survived and have been passed on. Falassi writes of the Veglia:

> La Veglia; the word and the custom that surrounds it have an old-fashioned ring to Tuscans today. Yet these fireside evenings and their homespun performances are not so far removed from contemporary people's experience, for it is only in the last decade or so that the occasion has lost its vitality. . . . The Veglia has lasted over 500 years without losing its function or meaning.

Traditionally, to attend a Veglia one had to be a member of the family; "of the blood" as they say. Other participants in the Veglia could be relatives "of the same blood" or those acquired through marriage. Throughout the Middle Ages the Veglia was held during the period of the year between the fall and winter sowing of the crops and Lent (even though the common rituals extended to cover the complete cycle of the year and all four seasons).

The fireside hearth was the center of the Italian Pagan's home, a place it has maintained for centuries. The family and the fireplace belonged to the mother of the home and it was she who tended the fire. In the center of the fireplace sat the "fire stone," a fireproof slab over which the fire burned. The umbilical cords of children born into the family were placed beneath the stone (a custom based on the folklore belief that this kept the family bonded together). This is an indication that the fire stone was an important element in the Veglia family gatherings.

Appendix 2

The Ancestral Lare Spirit

Lare are Ancestral spirits that protect and preserve family lines and family knowledge. They are the bridge to the past, connecting the present to all that has come before. In old practices a Lare shrine is set in the home, typically occupying the east or west quarter. They are traditionally spirits associated with the hearth, and many people place their Lare shrine on the mantle, or somewhere near the hearth.

In archaic Roman religion the Lare were worshipped at the crossroads where small towers were erected in their honor and offerings were placed on an altar set before them[1]. The Lare were originally spirits of the fields, and after the rise of agriculture they became associated with plots of farmland. In this aspect they guarded specific places, the towers erected in their honor being, in effect, their watchtowers. Because the Lare were associated with planting, they were also linked to the seasons and to time itself[2]. The Divine protection of places held as much meaning to the ancient Romans as did the protection of time and the seasons. The Roman god Janus stood at the threshold of all of these things, and was linked to the Lare through this relationship. He was also the god of doorways, and the Lare were spirits of the hearth and protectors of the

1   Dumezil, Georges. *Archaic Roman Religion* (vol. 1). Baltimore: John Hopkins University Press, 1996, pp. 343–344.
2   Dumezil, Georges. *Archaic Roman Religion* (vol. 1). Baltimore: John Hopkins University Press, 1996, pp. 340–346.

home. Here they joined together as household spirits. Because the Lare were also spirits of the seasons and of time, they were considered Ancestral spirits linking the past, present, and future together through preservation of lineage.

The Lare were associated with other protectors known as the Penates (pay-nah-tays) who were spirits that protected the food supply within the home. Our modern word *pantry* is derived from Penate. It is significant to note that the Lare provided indiscriminate protection of all members of the household, free or slave, blood related or not. As a result, the slave class and the lower free class in Rome found religious shelter in the Lare cult. Among modern Italian practitioners, non-Italians are adopted into the Clan through the Lare and thereby become full members of the tradition in all regards.

Because of their earliest connection to fields and meadows, the Lare also have a relationship with Faunus, Silvanus, and other rustic gods. With the rise of agriculture the Lare became linked to the seed. This resulted in a connection of the planted seed with the buried flesh. In death, the ancient Romans were more concerned with disappearance from this world than with entry into the next. To the Romans death was a defilement of the person, and this defilement had to be removed by the performance of certain rites. Specifically this required the sacrifice of a sow to Ceres, a sacred meal eaten at the burial site, and a ritual cleansing of the home of the departed. This evolved into the modern custom of the *wake meal* and the sending of flowers to the home.

In Roman religion a Divine force survived the departed man, and this was the *genius* spirit, a living entity passed from family to family through the head of the household. For the female this same force was called her *juno* spirit. The Genius (family spirit) connected to the father of the family was personified in art, linking him to the Ancestral spirit. This portrait introduced the genius to each new generation. On the center of the Lare shrine was a painting of the father flanked on each side by a Lare spirit. The female juno spirit was never depicted in art but was connected to the hearth. Here it was represented by the goddess Vesta, of whom no Roman statue was ever made. Vesta was the spirit of the fire within the hearth. The wife of the home was responsible for keeping the fire alive, just as vestal virgins kept the eternal flame alive in the temple of Vesta.

The juno spirit belonging to the wife was with her in everything that she performed. It was passed to her on the day of her marriage beneath her veil in a ceremony performed by a priest of Jupiter and Juno. Today this ancient connection lives on in the popularity of June weddings, the month sacred to Juno. A woman's juno gave her fertility and assisted in childbirth. Every woman had her juno, every man his genius sharing in all the aspects of their life.

Offerings at both the hearth and the Lare shrine were important duties. In archaic Roman religion, inherited from the Etruscans, spirits of the Dead known as *mane* lived on in or near their tombs, and had to be fed. When these spirits were satisfied, they were favorable towards the Living. But when neglected, they suffered and took vengeance on the Living, becoming the Lemures. In later times the custom of feeding the departed at their place of burial evolved into the placing of offerings such as spelt grain or cakes at the Lare shrine. These shrines depicted a serpent on the base, and in archaic Roman religion the Ancestral spirit came in the form of a serpent to take the offerings laid on the hearth[3].

---

3 Grenier, Albert. *The Roman Spirit in Religion, Thought, and Art.* New York: Alfred A. Knopf, 1926, pp. 94–95.

The Lare were always honored with special offerings and a lighted lamp whenever important family matters arose such as a birth, death, or marriage. The presence of these spirits in the daily life of the family and on important occasions bound the family together in a spiritual unity that went beyond the natural bonds of affection. The Lare represent a very ancient family cult that was born of the division of the various parts of the household. The hearth containing the fire essential for cooking and keeping warm, the pantry guarded by the Penates, and the head of the household who was heir of the genius of his forebearers now in the Otherworld all ensured the perpetuity of the race. Due to its great importance whenever the family moved, special care was taken to transport the Lare shrine to the new residence.

Bibliography

Allen, Richard Hinckley. *Star Names: Their Lore and Meaning.* New York: Dover Publications, 1963.

Briggs, Katharine. *The Vanishing People: Fairy Lore and Legend.* New York: Pantheon Books, 1978.

Butler, W.E. *Magic: Its Ritual, Power and Purpose.* New York: Samuel Weiser Inc., 1977.

Case, Paul Foster. *The Tarot: A Key to the Wisdom of the Ages.* Los Angeles: Builders of the Adytum, 1947.

Cousineau, Phil. *Once and Future Myths: The Power of Ancient Stories in Modern Times.* Berkeley: Conari Press, 2001.

Cumont, Franz. *After Life in Roman Paganism.* New York: Dover Publications, Inc., 1959.

Devereux, Paul. *Fairy Paths and Spirit Roads.* London: Chrysalis Books Group, 2003.

Eliade, Mircea. *The Myth of the Eternal Return.* Princeton, NJ: Princeton University Press, 2005.

Evans-Wentz, W.Y. *The Fairy Faith in Celtic Countries.* New York: Citadel Press, 1994.

Falassi, Alessandro. *Folklore by the Fireside: Text and Context of the Tuscan Veglia.* Austin: University of Texas Press, 1980.

Fortune, Dion. *Practical Occultism in Daily Life.* New York: Samuel Weiser Inc., 1966.

———. *Through the Gates of Death.* New York: Samuel Weiser Inc., 1968.

Foxwood, Orion. *The Faery Teachings.* Coral Springs: Muse Press, 2003.

———. *The Tree of Enchantment: Ancient Wisdom and Magic Practices of the Faery Tradition.* San Francisco: Weiser Books, 2008.

Gordon, Richard. "Imagining Greek and Roman Magic." In *Witchcraft and Magic in Europe,* edited by Bengt Ankarloo and Stuart Clark. Philadelphia: University of Pennsylvania, 1999.

Gray, William G. *Western Inner Workings.* York Beach: Samuel Weiser, Inc., 1983.

Grenier, Albert. *The Roman Spirit in Religion, Thought, and Art.* New York: Alfred A. Knopf, 1926.

Grimassi, Raven. *The Cauldron of Memory: Retrieving Ancestral Knowledge and Wisdom.* Woodbury: Llewellyn Publications, 2009.

Hall, Manly. *The Secret Teachings of All Ages.* Los Angeles: The Philosophical Research Society, Inc., 1973.

Harris, Mike. *The Quest of the Celtic Mysteries: Awen.* Oceanside: Sun Chalice Books, 1999.

Head, Joseph, and Cranston, S.L. *Reincarnation, an East–West Anthology.* New York: Aeon Publishing, 2000.

Henderson, Joseph, and Oakes, Maud. *The Wisdom of Serpent: The Myths of Death, Rebirth, and Resurrection.* Princeton, NJ: Princeton University Press, 1990.

Kerenyi, Karl. *Hermes: Guide of Souls.* Putnam: Spring Publications, 1976.

Kondratiev, Alexei. *A Path to Celtic Ritual: The Apple Branch.* New York: Citadel Press Books, 2003.

Lecouteux, Claude. *The Return of the Dead: Ghosts, Ancestors, and the Transparent Veil of the Pagan Mind.* Rochester: Inner Traditions, 2009.

———. *The Tradition of Household Spirits: Ancestral Lore and Practices.* Rochester: Inner Traditions, 2013.

MacEowen, Frank. *The Spiral of Memory and Belonging: A Celtic Path of Soul and Kinship.* Novato: New World Library, 2004.

McNeill, F. Marian. *The Silver Bough, Volume One: Scottish Folklore and Folk-Belief.* Glasgow: William MacLellan, 1977.

Narby, Jeremy. *The Cosmic Serpent: DNA and the Origins of Knowledge.* New York: Putnam, 1998.

Papon, Donald. *The Lure of the Heavens: A History of Astrology.* New York: Samuel Weiser, 1972.

Roney-Dougal, Serena. *The Faery Faith: An Integration of Science with Spirit.* London: Green Magic, 2003.

Sagan, Carl. *Shadows of Forgotten Ancestors.* New York: Ballantine Books, 1992.

Song, Tamarack. *Journey to the Ancestral Self.* Barrytown: Station Hill Press, 1994.

Spence, Lewis. *The Mysteries of Britain: The Secret Rites and Traditions of Ancient Britain Restored.* North Hollywood: Newcastle Publishing, 1993.

Stewart, R.J. *Earth Light: The Ancient Path to Transformation Rediscovering the Wisdom of Celtic Faery Lore.* Lake Toxaway: Mercury Publishing, 1998.

———. *Power within the Land: The Roots of Celtic and Underworld Traditions Awakening the Sleepers and Regenerating the Earth.* Shaftsbury: Element Books, 1992.

About the Author

Peter Paradise, Raven Wolfe Photography

Raven Grimassi is a Neo-Pagan scholar and award-winning author of numerous books, including *The Grimoire of the Thorn-Blooded Witch*. He is a member of the American Folklore Society and is co-founder and co-director of the Crossroads Fellowship, a modern Mystery School tradition.

Grimassi's background includes training in traditional witchcraft and contemporary systems including Brittic Wicca, the Pictish-Gaelic tradition, Celtic Traditionalist, and Stregheria. Raven was also a member of the Rosicrucian Order, and studied the Kabbalah through the First Temple of Tifareth under Lady Sara Cunningham. His early magical career began in the late 1960s and involved the study of works by Julius Evola, Franz Bardon, Gareth Knight, Kenneth Grant, Dion Fortune, William Gray, Austin Spare, William Butler, Israel Regardie, Eliphas Levi, and William Barrett.

You can visit Raven at *ravengrimassi.net*.

To Our Readers

Weiser Books, an imprint of Red Wheel/Weiser, publishes books across the entire spectrum of occult, esoteric, speculative, and New Age subjects. Our mission is to publish quality books that will make a difference in people's lives without advocating any one particular path or field of study. We value the integrity, originality, and depth of knowledge of our authors.

Our readers are our most important resource, and we appreciate your input, suggestions, and ideas about what you would like to see published.

Visit our website at *www.redwheelweiser.com* to learn about our upcoming books and free downloads, and be sure to go to *www.redwheelweiser.com/newsletter/* to sign up for newsletters and exclusive offers.

You can also contact us at info@rwwbooks.com or at
Red Wheel/Weiser, LLC
65 Parker Street, Suite 7
Newburyport, MA 01950